P9-AFF-518

California Desert

Byways

Backcountry drives
for the
whole family

By **TONY HUEGEL**

Cover design, maps, art and production
by Jerry Painter

Photography by Tony Huegel

Published by The Post Company
P.O. Box 1800, Idaho Falls, Idaho 83403

First edition
First printing, 1995
Second printing (revised), 1996

Produced in the United States of America.

Edited by Mei-Mei Chan
Cover design and maps by Jerry Painter

Library of Congress Number 94-073982
ISBN 0-9636560-3-1

Cover photo: Driving through the Joshua tree forest in Hidden Valley, Death Valley National Park.

Praise for Tony Huegel's series
Backcountry Drives for the Whole Family

"Author Tony Huegel has ... produced some of the best guides that we've ever seen for those who really want to get away with the whole family. *California Coastal Byways*, *California Desert Byways*, *Sierra Nevada Byways* and *Idaho Off-road* all offer concise directions, clear maps and excellent advice on how to get the most out of your off-road adventure."

MotorWeek ® (Maryland Public Television)

"Try some backcountry exploring using (*Utah Byways*) or other Byways Books. You won't be disappointed."

4Wheel Drive & Sport Utility Magazine

Disclaimer

This book has been prepared to help you and your family enjoy backcountry driving. However, it is not intended to be an exhaustive, all-encompassing authority on backcountry driving, nor is it intended to be your only source of information about backcountry driving. You must understand that there are risks and dangers that are inevitable when driving in the backcountry. If you drive the routes listed in this book, or any other backcountry roads, you assume all risks, dangers and liability that may result from your actions. The author and publisher of this book disclaim any and all liability for any injury, loss or damage that you, your passengers or your vehicle may incur.

Exercise the caution and good judgment that visiting the backcountry demands. Follow the guidelines in this book. Bring the proper supplies. Remember that the condition of backroads, especially those that are not paved, can and does change. Be prepared for accidents, injuries, breakdowns or other problems, because help is almost always far away.

Acknowledgments

No project of this sort is the product of one person's effort alone. Some people contributed by suggesting drives, others by reading the material and suggesting improvements and corrections. Others made the whole thing possible in the first place.

Among the latter are my publisher, Jerry Brady, and my editor, Mei-Mei Chan.

No one's support and cooperation was more important or fundamental than that of my wife, Lynn MacAusland, and our two children, Hannah and Land. They endured intense summer heat, high winds, dusty tenting, cramped quarters and even some danger while accompanying me during much of my research for this book. I couldn't be more grateful for their forbearance.

Roger Brandt, a ranger at Death Valley National Park, suggested drives. He also reviewed material for me, and contributed four drives that add greatly to the book's coverage of the park: Cottonwood & Marble canyons, Chloride City, Hole-In-The-Wall and Butte Valley.

Another Death Valley ranger, Kevin Emmerich, provided important information about the park.

Art Kidwell of Joshua Tree National Park reviewed my descriptions of the drives there.

Fred Jee of Anza-Borrego Desert State Park made valuable comments about portions of the manuscript and provided thoughtful insights into what the desert has to offer. Ernie Brown provided background about the Picacho State Recreation Area.

Quite a number of Bureau of Land Management officials also contributed, either by suggesting drives, critiquing parts of the manuscript, or researching and verifying information. They include: Jim Jennings, Cheryl Seath, Genivieve Rasmussen, Kirk Halford and Joe Pollini of the Bishop office; Tim Finger of the El Centro office; Dave Wash of the Ridgecrest office; David Frink of the Barstow office; and David Eslinger of the Palm Springs office. The staff at the California Desert Information Center in Barstow were helpful as well.

Kay Rohde, of the National Park Service, assisted with material for Mojave National Preserve.

Scott Sinclair, a knowledgeable off-highway touring enthusiast, provided background about the Mojave Road. But for information about that drive, I am particularly indebted to Dennis Casebier and the Friends of the Mojave Road, whose book Mojave Road Guide is an essential companion for anyone considering driving the historic route.

Howard Grice, of Inyo National Forest's White Mountain Ranger Station, has always been quick to provide assistance when needed.

I'm sure I've overlooked someone. That is unintentional and is not to suggest that their contributions were any less significant.

Contents

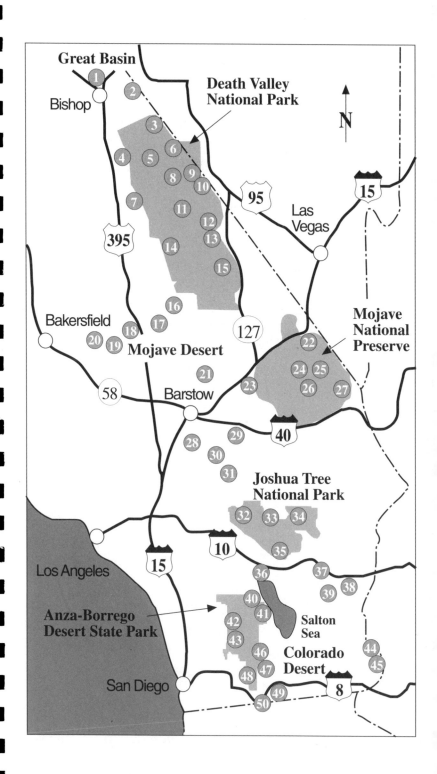

Great Basin

Bishop

Death Valley National Park

N

Las Vegas

95

15

395

Bakersfield

Mojave Desert

Mojave National Preserve

127

58

Barstow

40

28

29

30

31

Joshua Tree National Park

10

15

Los Angeles

Anza-Borrego Desert State Park

Salton Sea

Colorado Desert

San Diego

8

Appendix

Route descriptions

Saying a desert drive is fun, easy, hard, rough, long or short can be quite subjective. Much of that assessment depends on the individual's experience, likes and dislikes, perceptions and circumstances. I've tried to bring some objectivity to the categories I've used to describe each drive, but that can only go so far. Anyway, here's what's behind each category:

LOCATION: Where the drive is.

HIGHLIGHTS: What's best about the drive.

DIFFICULTY: This is subjective. I've assumed you are not a hard-core four-wheeler, but just somebody in a modern sport-utility vehicle who's looking for reasonably safe adventure. The ratings are: *easy*, which means it's a real cruise that probably won't require four-wheel drive; *moderate,* which means you'll need four-wheel drive occasionally, the going will be slow, and you can expect rough spots; and *difficult*, which means rough and slow, using four-wheel drive most or all of the time, and a higher likelihood that you'll scrape your undercarriage's protective skid plates on rocks. The latter moments are few in this book.

TIME & DISTANCE: The estimated time it takes to complete the drive, excluding your travel time getting to the starting point. The time element can vary enormously for each drive, depending on how much time you want to spend at stops along the way. Since odometer accuracy varies among vehicles, your measurements of distances might differ somewhat from mine. But they shouldn't differ much.

GETTING THERE: This will direct you to the starting point.

THE DRIVE: Details of the trip, such as what turns to take, where you'll end up, how far it is from here to there, and what you'll see along the way.

REST STOPS: Where you can stop for a picnic, to camp, buy a bite to eat, explore a ghost town, visit a museum, etc.

GETTING HOME: This will vary according to where home is. But there are usually common exit points leading to highways.

MAPS: Each trip recommends specific U.S. Bureau of Land Management Desert Access Guides and occasionally other maps. The maps are being revised to reflect the 1994 California Desert Protection Act, which made substantial changes in how the desert is managed, and by whom. Maps produced by AAA affiliate Automobile Club of Southern California (ACSC) are great. They are listed along with each route on page 150.

INFORMATION: A telephone number for road conditions or other information. In the back of the book is a list of BLM offices and other agencies in the region. **NOTE: Most of the telephone numbers with 619 area codes will change to area code 760 in March 1997.**

ALSO TRY: Other routes in the area, which may or may not be among the drives detailed in this book.

Map symbols

Points of interest	■	Road number	03
Paved road	——	Interstate highway	15
Easy dirt road	≈≈≈	U.S. highway	20
Primitive road	≈≈==≈	State highway	89
Camping	△	North indicator	↑ N
Lakes	◗		
Streams	～～		
Mountain	⌃⌃		
Ranger station	⬆		
Picnic area	⛉		
City or town	○		

Trips indicated in color

Paved road	～～
Easy dirt road	≈≈≈
Primitive road	≈≈≈≈

Guide for trip activities

Mt. biking

Wildlife viewing

Photo opportunities

Camping

Hiking

Historic sites

Petroglyphs

Picnicking

Restaurant

INTRODUCTION

The off-ramp to adventure

Escaping California's crowded highways and campgrounds has often meant standing in line for a wilderness permit, hauling a backpack, praying that the next hill goes down instead of up and that the kids will understand that this is play, not punishment.

No more. With so many people switching from sedans, station wagons and vans to sport-utility vehicles, California's wild and uncrowded places are more accessible than ever. Now families, physically disabled people, aging boomers, seniors — just about anyone with a few hours to spare — can drive the state's huge network of adventure backroads to the kind of places that used to be the domain of hikers, mountain bikers and serious four-wheelers.

California Desert Byways is your introduction to the unpaved alternatives in the spectacular region between the Owens Valley and the Mexican border. With a factory-stock SUV you'll be able to leave the highways and explore deep gorges, ancient archaeological sites, remote valleys and towering mountain ranges that relatively few people ever see up close.

The routes I describe are either entirely unpaved, or substantially so. They range from well-graded dirt and gravel roads that are easy in two-wheel drive, to more rugged two-track trails that will require the 4x4 capabilities built into your SUV. While some involve major detours from main highways, others are just a short distance from major interstate freeways, making them ideal side trips. All are established routes open to public use. They are arranged essentially north to south.

Choosing unpaved, often remote and rugged roads through publicly owned lands is much like choosing hiking trails instead of concrete sidewalks. They get us closer to nature and history, to what remains of the Wild West, and to ourselves. They take us far from crowds, traffic and noise. They offer adventure, solitude, excitement and even challenges that help break up the routines of daily life.

California Desert Byways tells you where to go, and how to get there and back while preserving the qualities that make unspoiled places worth visiting. You'll also learn something about the geology and history of these places. Now and then I even mention good places in town to eat and sleep.

With the help of *California Desert Byways*, part of my series of guidebooks covering California's backcountry roads, you will discover a new side of a state that seems never to run out of surprises.

— *Tony Huegel*

The California Desert:
Wasteland or wonderland?

"The real voyage of discovery consists not in seeking new landscapes but in having new eyes."

Marcel Proust

The desert, vast and still, spread out below me as I drove toward the Bradshaw Trail from the Chuckwalla Mountains. It was a July afternoon, the time of day and year that gives the desert its fearsome reputation. The landscape shimmered in the heat. Living things were hunkered down, just trying to survive.

I stopped to scan the courses of several spurs. Do I go left? Right? Suddenly, the incongruous brilliance of a tiny purple flower caught my eye. Normally, desert flowers bloom in the kinder temperatures and gentler sunshine of spring, after the parched soil has been quenched by winter rains. But this delicate little thing, about the size of a quarter, had defied the punishing heat and bravely bloomed in the tenuous shade of an upended stone.

I climbed out of my family-style 4x4, got down on my belly, and admired it. It made me realize that even in the harsh conditions of summer there is life and beauty in the desert, a place that is simultaneously threatening and inviting, brutal and sublime.

Many people have long viewed the California Desert as a wasteland. To some it has seemed the perfect place to bomb, dump or otherwise destroy for economic, military or recreational purposes. Others have viewed it as an almost lifeless place to be "reclaimed" with water shipped from far away at great financial and environmental cost. But it can seem a wasteland only if one fails to look closely.

Beauty here is subtle and spare. Rainfall averages a scant two to five inches a year. Summer temperatures often soar well above 100° F. Life is pared down to its essentials. Seemingly empty and silent expanses belie the presence of complex and dynamic ecosystems and powerful, active geologic forces. Thus, for many of us, appreciating desert lands is an acquired skill. For instance, we scowl at the bleached and sterile face of the desert when the sun is high. But do we notice how that face changes in late afternoon and through early evening? Then, when the sun is low, it suffuses the desert with a rich golden hue. Shadows are cast. The texture of every plant, the subtle undulations of the land, the grain of the rocks and the silhouettes of jagged mountain peaks are revealed. In summer, the drab mountains and flats appear monotonous. Yet in spring, after good winter rains, the desert can become a gallery of wildflowers.

Encompassing about 25 million acres, extending 375 miles north to south and 275 miles east to west at its midsection, the California Desert is the largest expanse of publicly owned land in the state. About three million acres are set aside as military reserves. About 14 million acres have been designated as protected wilderness areas. There are 90 mountain ranges, perhaps more than 100,000 archaeological sites as well as wetlands, waterfalls, lava flows, caverns and gorges. About half a million people call it home.

The desert also is home to hundreds of species of plants and animals that have adapted to a life of scarcity. There are bighorn sheep, cougars, tortoises, raptors, cholla cactus gardens and forests of Joshua trees. Jackrabbits, which love to dart out in front of cars from behind bushes, seem to be everywhere. (The kids will enjoy counting them.) You'll see roadrunners sprinting along the roadsides. In Afton Canyon, where the Mojave River provides rare year-round surface water, you might see an eagle. Sometimes, as in the case of the threatened desert tortoise, animals that have for ages successfully endured some of the harshest conditions in North America are struggling to survive the encroachment of man and other factors that put their continued existence at risk.

The California Desert is really three intriguing deserts: the Great Basin, the Mojave and the Colorado (Sonoran). From the massive peaks that tower over the Owens Valley in the north to the narrow gorges and palm oases of the Colorado Desert in the south, the region is a place of spectacular contrasts and extremes.

The Owens Valley is a confluence of sorts, where the Sierra Nevada Mountains, the Great Basin Desert and the Mojave Desert meet. The mountainous, sagebrush-covered Great Basin enters California from Nevada at the northern end of the valley (and in the far northeastern corner of the state, an area that is not covered in this book). It is high desert, mostly 4,000 feet above sea level or higher. Winters are colder there than in the other two deserts. The White Mountains, where White Mountain Peak rises to 14,246 feet, and the Inyo Mountains, a connected range to the south, form the highest range in the Great Basin and the eastern wall of the Owens Valley. The valley's western wall is formed by one of the world's steepest escarpments, the dramatic eastern side of the High Sierra, the largest single mountain range in the Lower 48. There, the tallest peak in the contiguous states, Mt. Whitney, rises to 14,495 above sea level. The valley itself, called a graben in geologic terms, has subsided and stretched as the mountains flanking it have risen. It now lies some 10,000 feet below the highest peaks around it.

The Owens Valley and the White-Inyo Mountains occupy the rain shadow of the Sierra. Eastbound Pacific air arrives in the valley sapped of moisture after its journey up the western slope and over the crest of the mountains. While precipitation on the western slope has averaged as high as 50 inches a year, east of the crest rainfall averages a scant 5 to 15 inches a year. Since the early 1900s, when the city of Los Angeles began appropriating the water of the Owens Valley, people have made it even drier, just as we've made other desert places bloom through irrigation.

The region extending east from the Sierra, location of the southernmost active glacier in the United States, to the parched floor of Death Valley is a landscape that is unsurpassed in natural beauty, climatic variety, geologic scale and, importantly, accessibility. In the morning you can leave your campsite in the High Sierra, drive east through the geologic waves of basin and range desert, plunge into Death Valley, head west again through Panamint Valley, and be back at your mountain retreat before sundown.

The Mojave Desert spreads eastward like a fan from the juncture of the Tehachapi Mountains, at the southern tip of the Sierra, and the San Gabriel Mountains. Most of the Mojave is in California. The newly designated, 1.4-million-acre Mojave National Preserve in the eastern part of the state is its geographic center. Its most recognizable symbol is the Joshua tree, which reminded early desert travelers of the prophet Joshua's outstretched arms. In the upper Mojave, elevations range between 2,000 and 4,000 feet. The lower Mojave drops to 282 feet below sea level at Badwater Basin in Death Valley, the lowest point in the western hemisphere.

Joshua Tree National Park lies on the dividing line between the ecosystems of the Mojave and Colorado deserts. The Colorado, or Sonoran, Desert encompasses much of southeastern California and most of Sonora in northern Mexico. This is low desert; most of it is well below 2,000 feet. Winters are mild. Summers are extremely hot. Incongruous bodies of water like the Colorado River, the great man-made canals and aqueducts, and the Salton Sea create peculiar sights in this particularly hot and exceedingly dry place.

Human beings have occupied the California Desert for tens of thousands of years, and it is common to see evidence of ancient desert dwellers juxtaposed with that of relative newcomers. Sometimes the contrast between what the ancients left behind and what we've been leaving behind for the last century is disturbing. Sometimes it shows how far we've come, how much easier life is for us than it was for our forebears. In other cases it shows how much we have to learn.

For example, at Steam Well, a small canyon near Red Mountain that is now protected by the new 37,700-acre Golden Valley Wilderness, the rubbish of an old mine lies at the base of cliffs decorated with petroglyphs, designs that were etched thousands of years ago into the iron-colored varnish that covers exposed desert rock. Not far away is a trash pile with old mattresses, tires and such that also is within the wilderness boundary. At Inscription Canyon near Barstow, a fine place to view ancient rock art, a visitor will notice that Albert Einstein apparently wasn't the first to develop that famous equation after all, for there it is, etched into the varnish alongside many mysterious symbols created by Native Americans ages ago. Along the Titus Canyon drive, in Death Valley National Park, you can visit the remains of the mining town of Leadfield, a relic of an attempt by transients to exploit the desert, and the Klare Spring petroglyphs, the art of people for whom the desert was home. Northeast of Barstow, just off the Yellow Brick Road to Las Vegas called Interstate 15, a budding archaeologist can explore the Calico Early Man Site, a prehistoric workshop, quarry and campsite that appears to be in need of every dollar of support it can get.

The California Desert Protection Act

Human beings and the California Desert have been adversaries in many ways for a very long time. Yet, to a significant degree, man is now the arbiter of the desert's fate.

In 1984 a number of conservation groups formed the California Desert Protection League. Its goal was to protect the desert from abuse and destruction by mining, off-highway vehicle use and other activities.

In 1986 then-U.S. Sen. Alan Cranston (D-Calif.) sought to accomplish that goal by introducing the California Desert Protection Act. That spurred creation of the California Desert Coalition, an umbrella group of mining interests, ranchers, off-highway vehicle users, some local governments and others who felt the bill ignored the concerns and interests of traditional desert users and desert residents. They hoped either to kill the legislation, or to minimize its impact.

The legislation didn't pass until October 1994, in the final hours of the 103rd Congress. But passage came only after compromises were reached, and after it became caught up in the hard-fought Senate race between its principal sponsor, Sen. Dianne Feinstein, D-Calif., and her challenger, Rep. Michael Huffington, R-Calif. President Bill Clinton subsequently signed the bill into law.

In a single stroke it set aside the largest amount of land for wilderness and parks ever in the lower 48 states, adding about 7.7 million acres of new federal wilderness to the 6.3 million acres previously designated in California.

Death Valley National Monument, which encompassed more than two million acres, was made a national park. With the new designation came an additional 1.3 million acres previously managed by the U.S. Bureau of Land Management. Of the park's total acreage, more than 3.1 million are now designated as federally protected wilderness areas. The expansion made it the largest national park in the continental United States, more than a million acres larger than Yellowstone National Park. Areas like Darwin Falls, a rare year-round desert waterfall, and remote Saline and Eureka valleys, grabens like Owens and Death valleys, were added to the park.

Joshua Tree National Monument also became a national park. It was expanded by 234,000 acres, for a total of almost 794,000 acres. Of that, 132,000 acres are wilderness.

The status of the beautiful East Mojave National Scenic Area was upgraded to a 1.4-million-acre national preserve, with 695,000 wilderness acres. Management responsibility was transferred from the BLM to the National Park Service.

The law also created a desert lily preserve, protected dinosaur tracks, added Last Chance Canyon to Red Rock Canyon State Park, and withdrew 6,000 acres adjacent to Bodie State Historic Park from mining and mineral leasing.

Some rugged areas once enjoyed by serious off-roaders are now closed. But the typical person who drives a factory-stock sport-utility vehicle will likely see little change in the number and quality of places to go. For example, the law only eliminated two drives from the list of routes I had hoped to include in this book (the Steam Well petroglyph site, and Davies Valley west of El Centro). They were easily replaced.

Whether one wants more of the region open to four-wheeling, hunting, mining or similar uses, or set aside as places where natural and cultural values will be protected from abuse and destruction, the California Desert is a treasure that belongs to the nation, not just to Californians, and to future generations, not just to us.

I hope this book enables you to see and appreciate what all the commotion was about. I hope that you will use the book and your vehicle to experience the desert in a manner that will do no damage and cause no injury to yourself and your passengers. Ultimately, perhaps you will be able to decide for yourself whether the California Desert is a wasteland, a wonderland, or something in between.

Adventure motoring
in the California Desert

Touring the remote, unpaved backroads of the California Desert is a unique experience that can be done safely and responsibly. But you must take the necessary precautions and use good judgment to avoid injury to yourself and your passengers, and damage to the environment and your vehicle.

Here are some tips that will help you have a safe and rewarding experience:

KNOW WHERE YOU'RE GOING. The maps in this book are not intended for navigation. They are only at-a-glance maps to give you a general idea of where the drives are. For greater detail and navigational purposes, I generally recommend U.S. Bureau of Land Management maps, called Desert Access Guides. They're good all–round maps for this purpose. They include explanations of interesting places, and are color-keyed to identify public and private lands, which will help you avoid trespassing. Some include contour lines similar to those on topographic maps. There are 22 of them, covering the desert region from just east of Bishop to the Mexican border. Good as they are, they were somewhat out of date even before the California Desert Protection Act became federal law in the fall of 1994, designating millions of acres as protected wilderness areas that are now off–limits to mechanized travel. They are currently $4 each and can be purchased at BLM offices and information centers, or ordered from the California Desert District Office at the address in the back of this book. Outdoor equipment stores carry U.S. Geological Survey topographic maps that show elevations and more detail. You might have to buy more than one for each trip, so they can become expensive. AAA affiliate Automobile Club of Southern California has excellent maps that I've found to be very useful in finding and exploring backcountry byways. They are free to members.

Whichever maps you choose, study them before you leave. Learn your route before you start out. Bring the maps with you. Keep close track of where you've been along the way, and be aware of what's to come.

BE CAREFUL. The best advice is to not travel alone. There's no security like more than one vehicle. But the reality is that when you're on vacation, or off for a day or weekend, you'll probably have little choice but to go alone.

I believe that backcountry travel can be done safely, even alone, with proper precautions, preparation and due recognition of the potential hazards. Some of the roads in this book are about as safe and easy as roads can be, even though they are unpaved. Others are rudimentary two-tracks. Some are even popular, so you may have company.

Consider the time of day before you set out. Is it getting late? Don't get caught out there at night.

While the desert can be interesting in summer, temperatures are often well into the triple digits. The risk of a serious mishap is higher then as well. Very few people venture into the desert in summer, making help much harder to find. Sand can be especially soft, deep and treacherous when it loses its moisture to heat and wind. Just as wet sand at the beach is easier to walk on, desert sand with some moisture in it provides a firmer roadbed.

The best times to visit the desert are from late fall through early spring, depending on where you go. But realize that many high-desert places, particularly the mountains, get snow in winter. Some roads and high passes, like North and South passes on the Saline Valley Road, can be closed in winter. Spring seems to be everyone's favorite time to visit the desert, for good reason. Temperatures then are ideal, typically in the 50s at night and 80s during the day depending on the elevation. Desert vegetation is green. Best of all, if the previous winter has been a wet one, the desert can erupt with magnificent wildflower displays, with the timing depending on the elevation. Anza-Borrego Desert State Park even has a wildflower hotline you can call. (It's listed with the addresses and telephone numbers in the back of this book.) If you go in summer, which modern air conditioning makes feasible, head for the higher and cooler places. Much of Death Valley National Park, for example, is thousands of feet above sea level and not so notoriously hot.

Always carry lots of water. Sweet, sugary drinks like soda pop will not do the job. And drink often, even if you don't feel thirsty. You will dry out in the desert, and the serious effects of dehydration can creep up on you before you realize what's happening. Even if you're just taking a short walk, carry water and wear a hat. Ground temperatures are far hotter than air temperatures in summer.

Always be prepared to spend a few days out there, in case you get stuck or lost, or your vehicle breaks down. Carry adequate survival supplies for the number of people you have along. Bring a tarp and poles to make shade if necessary.

Don't be tempted by excessively steep, rocky or sandy stretches. Know your vehicle. Don't overestimate what it can do. Many 4x4 owners will admit that they never got stuck so often or so badly before they bought a vehicle they thought could go anywhere. Always remember that help can be a long way off, especially in the desert. Wear your seat belt. Have children in proper safety restraints. Always check the weather forecast before setting out, and watch for changes. Be mindful of the flash-flood potential, especially in mid- to late-summer when subtropical air from northern Mexico and the Gulf of California can produce sudden downpours. Even if the rain falls miles away, the cloudbursts can send massive amounts of water, rock and mud crashing down canyons and desert washes that just moments before were serene and dry. Watch the skies. If rain clouds begin to form, turn back. If you can't, retreat quickly to the highest ground you can find.

Before you set out check with the appropriate land management agency, such as park or Bureau of Land Management officials, for the latest road conditions. They have knowledgeable people, and wind and water can change the condition, even the course, of a route, especially if it involves a wash. When you finish the drive, let them know how it went so they'll have the latest information for the next person.

FOLLOW THE RULES. There are some, written and unwritten, even in places where it's likely no one will be looking. The intent behind them is to keep you safe. They also help to preserve these places from the kind of abuse and destruction that disturbs wildlife, interferes with other lawful uses like livestock grazing, or damages the environment and archaeological and historic sites. Misconduct and mistakes can result in personal injury, damage to your vehicle, areas being closed, and possible legal penalties.

• Your vehicle must be fully street legal to take these drives. You must obey all traffic laws.

• Never drive in designated wilderness areas, which are usually marked with signs. Go only where motorized vehicles are permitted. You must always remain on established routes designated for motor vehicle use. Never make a new trail, or follow in the tracks of some irresponsible person who did. Mechanized travel, including on motorcycles and mountain bikes, is not allowed in wilderness areas unless a legal route for such travel has been designated. There are several such routes in this book.

• Obey regulatory and private property signs.

• Do not touch, collect, remove or in any way disturb such ancient cultural treasures as petroglyphs or geoglyphs. They are protected by federal and state laws. View them from a distance. Do not use archaeological sites for picnics or camping. The more time people spend at these sites, the greater the likelihood of damage. The same goes for old mines, homesteads, ghost towns and similar sites. Some historic sites, like the ghost town of Cerro Gordo in the Inyo Mountains, are private property. The National Park Service in particular prohibits removing anything at all from lands they manage. Camping and campfires on those lands are restricted to fireplaces in designated campgrounds. Gathering firewood is prohibited. On BLM lands, including wilderness, gathering firewood is limited to dead and down materials. Live vegetation cannot be cut. But you really should bring your own wood. The desert has little to spare, and even dead wood is important to desert ecosystems. If you make a fire, keep it small. Use existing fire rings. If you go with a group, make only one fire.

• Give someone a copy of your map showing the routes you plan to take. Let the person know when you'll return, and whom to call if you don't. Be sure to check in with that person when you return. Invite a friend to come along in his or her vehicle if you can.

• Camp only in established campsites, whether developed or primitive.

• Don't disturb wildlife or livestock. Leave gates as you find them.

• Leave no trace of your visit. Take out only what you bring in. Clean up after yourself and those who came before you.

• Be extremely careful around old mining operations. They're very dangerous, especially for children. View them from a distance. Never enter shafts, tunnels or holes.

• Avoid parking on grass; hot exhaust systems can ignite fires. Avoid steep hillsides, stream banks and meadows.

• If you get stuck or lost, it's crucial that you stay with your vehicle. It'll be easier to find than you will be if you're walking through the mountains or desert. It will provide shelter, too.

• Remember that the miners, loggers and settlers who carved roads through the mountains, forests and deserts of the West over the last century didn't have your safety in mind. Spurs from the main roads can be very rough. If the going does get real rough, ask yourself if it's worth the risk to you, your passengers and your vehicle. Believe me, it's not.

Local four-wheel drive clubs sometimes offer clinics where you can learn off-highway driving skills. You might contact or join Tread Lightly!, Inc., an organization founded to promote environmentally responsible use of off-highway vehicles. It is based in Ogden, Utah. Call 1–800–966–9900.

BE PREPARED. Here's a checklist of some things to bring that you can adapt to suit your own needs.

❑ Food and cold drinks. Bring at least a gallon of water per day per person and an additional five gallons or so for your vehicle.

❑ Always start with a full fuel tank; carry several gallons of extra fuel in a full, well–sealed container.

❑ A good first aid kit, with plenty of ointment and bandages for the inevitable scraped knees and elbows.

❑ Very good tires, a good spare and jack, tire sealant, air pump, pressure gauge, and a small board to support the jack on dirt. You should also bring two sturdy boards, each about three feet long and at least as wide as your tires, to use for traction in case you become stuck in sand. If you need new tires anyway, buy moderately oversized tires. They'll give you better traction and flotation.

❑ Supplies, like sleeping bags and warm clothing, for spending the night in case you must. Nighttime temperatures in the desert can drop by 50 degrees from daytime highs, and can be quite cool in fall, winter and spring.

❑ In case you run into trouble, bring some basic tools, including jumper cables, duct tape, electrical tape, baling wire, spare fuses, multi-purpose knife, high-strength tow strap, fire extinguisher, shovel and a plastic sheet to put on the ground. An assortment of screws, washers, nuts, hose clamps and such could come in handy, too.

❑ Maps, compass
❑ Extra eyeglasses and keys
❑ Camera (still or video), film or video tape, tripod, binoculars
❑ Litter bag
❑ Flashlight or head lamp, extra batteries
❑ Matches and firewood
❑ Roadside emergency reflectors, flares, windshield scraper
❑ Reflective space blanket, useful in treating shock and highly visible to searching aircraft
❑ Altimeter, just for fun
❑ Watch
❑ Hats and clothing suitable to possible adverse weather
❑ Sunscreen and insect repellent
❑ Toilet paper, paper towels, wet wipes

I keep much of this stuff ready to go in one of those large plastic carryall containers you can buy just about anywhere. I'm often out alone scouting new drives, so sometimes I bring my mountain bike in case I get into a serious bind. I also use it to scout places that might damage my vehicle. If you do a lot of this stuff, think about getting a CB radio, even though their usefulness is limited. A cellular telephone might be handy, too.

I also have some tips on what to wear.

Forget shorts. Why would anyone expose his or her legs to brush, rocks, bugs, drying air and burning sun? Loose cotton pants and a loose cotton shirt, with breast pockets and sleeves you can roll up or down as needed, are best. I also recommend high-topped leather boots with lug soles. If you're like me, you're going to do a lot of scrambling around to get that perfect camera angle. Ankle-high boots let debris in. Always wear a hat outdoors in hot, sunny weather.

LEARN THE NECESSARY SKILLS. There are some driving techniques that can help you get where you're going and back again safely while avoiding environmental damage.

• Try not to spin your tires, which digs up the earth and could get you stuck.

• Learn how to work your four-wheel-drive system before setting out. Think ahead as you drive; engage 4wd before you actually need it. When in doubt, scout ahead. Walk uncertain stretches of trail before you drive them.

• Many times you'll find that your low-range gears will provide both greater control and the high engine revs you need at slow speeds. I use mine a lot. Use them to climb or descend steep hills and to inch through the inevitable tight spots without stalling. Avoid traversing steep hillsides if you can. Even if the road goes that way, use good judgment and stop if you're not confident it's safe. Don't try to turn around on a steep hillside. Back out. When climbing a steep hill, or going through mud, snow or sand, don't stop midway. Doing so could mean lost traction and stalling. Momentum can be everything, so keep moving. If you do stall going up a hill and must get out of the vehicle, put it in low-range first gear or reverse, and set the parking brake. Solidly block the wheels. When you try to get going again, play the parking brake against the clutch so you don't roll backwards. If you must back down a steep hill, put your vehicle in low-range reverse for greater control. Also use low-range to ease yourself down loose terrain. If your engine bogs down often in high range, switch to low range.

Remember that vehicles driving uphill have the right of way, if practical, because it's usually easier and safer for the vehicle going downhill to back up the hill.

• Have someone guide you through difficult spots. If the road has deep ruts, straddle them, letting them pass beneath the vehicle while the wheels ride high on the sides. Check your vehicle's clearance before driving over obstacles. Don't let rocks and such hit the big round parts, sometimes called "pumpkins," of your front and rear axles. Cracking or punching a hole in one will let vital oil drain out and expose the gears to dust and dirt. Run a tire over the obstacle if it's not too large, rather than letting it pass beneath your vehicle. Cross obstacles at an angle, rather than head–on.

• Avoid crossing streams if you can so you don't stir up the streambed. If you must cross a stream, do so only at an established crossing. Inspect streams closely before crossing. I pack a stick for checking the depth, comparing the depth to my vehicle. Cross slowly. Do not attempt to cross a road or streambed during a flood.

• If you must cross soft material such as sand, lower your vehicle's tire pressure to 15 pounds or so. That provides a larger footprint and greater flotation. The problem is that if a service station is far off, you'll need either a hand pump or a small electric air compressor, like those available at department stores, to get your tires back up to proper inflation when you return to pavement. It's important in sand to maintain your vehicle's momentum. If you must go through soft sand, keep up some speed so you can plow through it. You'll probably want to use your high-range gears, if your engine has adequate power.

• If you get stuck, don't panic. Calmly analyze the situation. With thought and work, you'll probably get out. Don't spin your tires if you get bogged down. That'll dig you in deeper. Try this: Jack up the vehicle and backfill the hole beneath the stuck tire with sand, building a base high enough to help you get a rolling start, then dampen the sand with water for firmer footing. Lower the vehicle and remove the jack. If you get high–centered, meaning your undercarriage is lodged on something high and your tires have daylight between them and the ground, take out your jack and the little board you brought to set it on. Carefully jack up the vehicle, little by little, placing rocks, dirt and other materials under each suspended tire to build a base for it to rest on.

• If you reach a point where there are several routes to choose from and none has a sign, follow what appears to be the most heavily used route.

• When going through rocks or rutted stretches, keep your hands loose on the steering wheel, at 10 and 2 o'clock. Keep your thumbs on top of the wheel. If a front tire hits a rock or rut, the steering wheel could suddenly be jerked in an unexpected direction, possibly injuring a thumb with a steering wheel spoke.

READ. You'll enjoy your desert adventures much more if you know something about the geology, flora, fauna and history of the region. Bookstores, visitor centers and other places have many fine titles to choose from. This book is not intended to be an exhaustive guide to exploring the desert.

HAVE FUN! You can easily justify the expense of a sport-utility vehicle, especially in a state with so much beautiful public land. And as you travel the backcountry, tell me what you've found, whether it's mistakes in the book or additional trips and tips you'd like to see added in future editions. Write to me in care of the Post Register, P.O. Box 1800, Idaho Falls, ID, 83403.

Making it fun for all

Trying to keep kids, especially teenagers, happy on car trips is a challenge. But there are many things you can do to make touring the desert as fun and interesting for them as it is for you.

Probably the best advice I can give is this: Don't just drive. Stop, and stop often.

Watch for wildlife. You'll see countless jackrabbits on some of these routes. They seem to play at darting into your path from behind a roadside bush. Get the kids to count them. You'll often see those most adaptable wild creatures, coyotes, as well. Look for animal tracks in the sand.

Trips that include ghost towns, old cabins, ancient petroglyphs and such will be big hits.

Bring a magnifying glass. Inspect and smell the wildflowers, the insects, the different types of rocks and trees. (Don't let them touch the cacti!) There's nothing like running your hand over the exposed wood of a western bristlecone pine that's as ancient as the pyramids, or across the layers of ancient sea bed sediments in the walls of a remote gorge. Get some good books on identifying wildflowers, birds, insects, rocks, vegetation and animals in the region. Get books on the geology and history of the area. They're available at local bookstores and visitor centers.

Make a photocopy of the area on the map where you'll be going. Get each child an inexpensive compass. Let them help you navigate and identify peaks, creeks, mine sites and other landmarks.

Let each child pack his or her favorite books and toys, but don't cram the car with stuff.

Bring at least one personal cassette player. Before leaving, go to your local public library and check out some children's cassette tapes. Better yet, buy some. You'll make good use of them for years to come.

Books on tape, something I listen to myself on long highway drives, are great diversions for children, too. Many video rental stores carry them.

Other items that have bought us quiet and good humor in the back seat are an inexpensive point-and-shoot camera the kids can use, and inexpensive binoculars. Now and then my son likes to have a notebook and pencil so he can pretend he's taking notes about our journeys just like dad.

If you have a responsible, licensed teenage driver on board, let him or her drive the safer and easier stretches. The sooner a teen learns backcountry driving skills, the longer he or she will remain an eager participant. And some day you may need an experienced co–pilot.

Of course, you must bring snacks, preferably the nutritious, non–sticky kind, and refreshing drinks. (Soda pop is not the best thirst quencher, especially if the weather is hot.) Be sure cups have secure tops that you can poke straws through. Plastic garbage bags, paper towels, changes of clothing and wet wipes are good to have along, too.

Safety is always a concern. Never let children wander around old buildings, or get close to old mines. The latter are especially dangerous.

Whether you travel with children or not, don't make the drive everything. Make it part of a day that draws on the huge range of experiences the California Desert has to offer.

Plan a picnic. See the sights. Hike to some hilltop. Bring your mountain bikes. And don't forget pillows for the sleepy. Finally, do something civilized when the drive is over: Go out to dinner.

Author's favorites

This is probably the most subjective section of this book. How does someone decide that one massive mountain range is more beautiful than another, one deep valley more appealing than another, or one narrow, high-walled gorge more intriguing than all the rest? I have no formula, just personal reactions to what I experience. No doubt you will make your own choices. Still, for what it's worth, here are some of my favorite routes.

Inyo Mountains — The views of the dramatic eastern slope of the Sierra Nevada Mountains, the Owens Valley, the basin and range country to the east and the Inyos themselves are truly breathtaking. Add to that the adrenaline of a few spots along the route that can be a bit challenging, though not difficult. For experienced backcountry drivers.

Jawbone to Lake Isabella — Absolutely stunning vistas as you climb up the eastern side of the Sierras, making the transition from the Mojave Desert to pine forests. Pastoral Kelso Valley is reminiscent of old California. More incredible views as you descend down switchbacks toward the lake.

Owens Valley to Death Valley — One of the two best ways to get to the new national park, in my view. You won't be stuck behind many lumbering RVs or timid tourists on this easy road through some of the remotest, most spectacular scenery in the West. The massive Eureka Sand Dunes, the Great Basin's highest, are not to be missed. All but 31 miles of the 110-mile route are on a narrow paved road.

Saline Valley Road — The second of the two best ways to get to Death Valley National Park. Like the Owens Valley to Death Valley Road, it starts out at the base of the snowy Sierras, then rises and falls as it takes you through the waves of basin and range country into remote Saline Valley and vast Panamint Valley. You can add the Hidden Valley and Racetrack Road drives. There are clothing-optional hot springs, with camping, in Saline Valley, most of which is now in the park.

Sandstone Canyon — If you only have time for one drive in Anza-Borrego Desert State Park, I say this is the one to take. The varied, primeval scenery is outstanding. Highlights include Split Mountain, with its strange anticline (layered rock bent by enormous geologic pressure), wind caves and narrow, high-walled Sandstone Canyon itself.

THE
DRIVES

Descending into Saline Valley on the Saline Valley Road.

The High Sierra across the Owens Valley from Mazourka Peak.

Volcanic Tableland

LOCATION: North of Bishop between U.S. 395 & U.S. 6, at the southern edge of the Great Basin Desert.

HIGHLIGHTS: Petroglyphs; Red Rock Canyon; vistas.

DIFFICULTY: Easy to moderate. Best late spring and fall.

TIME & DISTANCE: 50 miles; 3.5 hours.

GETTING THERE: I start at Bishop, but you can go the opposite way, beginning at Tom's Place on U.S. 395 northwest of Bishop. From Bishop, take U.S. 6 for 1.4 miles. Turn left (north) onto Five Bridges Road. Set your odometer at 0 here. Drive 2.4 miles through a gravel yard. After crossing a canal turn right (north) onto Fish Slough Road, No. 3V01.

THE DRIVE: This arid landscape formed 700,000 years ago when volcanic vents to the northwest spewed clouds of hot rhyolitic ash and rock particles that fused into rock formations. Visit Fish Slough, a wetland that supports plants and animals with water from the only natural springs remaining on the floor of Owens Valley. About 6.9 miles from where you turned onto Fish Slough Road, pull into the parking area to the left, walk to the rocks ahead and visit the grinding holes and petroglyphs. Four miles farther you'll see, on the right after you drop into Chidago Canyon, more petroglyphs behind a protective wire fence. There are more in another 5.85 miles, on the rocks to the left (west). In another 0.4 mile, go left (west) at the intersection, onto road 3S53. Soon you'll enter narrow Red Rock Canyon. When you exit the canyon and reach an intersection marked "Chidago Loop," go straight for 2.65 miles, then turn left (east) onto road 4S41, which will soon become a somewhat rough single-lane road as it climbs up a hillside. When you reach a saddle and you're facing the White Mountains, go right. Follow the road down a rocky pitch. After 1.2 miles you'll reach an intersection with the two-track road to Casa Diablo Mine and road 3S02. You can drive southeast 19 miles to Bishop on easy 3S02/4S04, Casa Diablo Road. Better yet, take 3S02 north for 6.35 miles through a pretty canyon to Benton Crossing Road. Turn left (west) toward the Sierra, then south on 4S02 toward U.S. 395.

REST STOPS: Cafe at Tom's Place; in Bishop, funky Bishop Grill for breakfast; excellent Whiskey Creek for dinner. Bishop has a great park; charming Elms Motel is next to it.

GETTING HOME: U.S. 395 north or south.

MAP: Inyo National Forest, 1993 edition.

INFORMATION: BLM in Bishop, 619-872-4881.

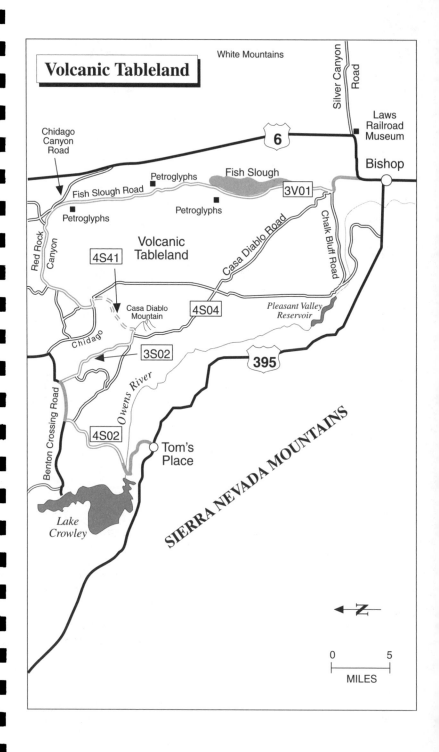

Volcanic Tableland

White Mountains

Silver Canyon Road

Laws Railroad Museum

6

Bishop

Chidago Canyon Road

Petroglyphs

Fish Slough

Fish Slough Road

3V01

Petroglyphs

Petroglyphs

Red Rock Canyon

Volcanic Tableland

4S41

Casa Diablo Road

Chalk Bluff Road

Casa Diablo Mountain

4S04

Pleasant Valley Reservoir

Chidago

3S02

395

Benton Crossing Road

Owens River

4S02

Tom's Place

SIERRA NEVADA MOUNTAINS

Lake Crowley

←N

0   5
MILES

White Mountains Loop

LOCATION: Inyo and Mono counties; east of Bishop.

HIGHLIGHTS: Ancient bristlecone pines, among the oldest living things on Earth; California's third-highest peak, White Mountain Peak (14,246 ft.) in the state's second–highest range; vistas of the High Sierra; Silver Canyon Road.

DIFFICULTY: Easy. But steep and narrow Silver Canyon Road will keep your hands cemented to the steering wheel. (I'll rate it moderate.) You can take the paved road up and enjoy the wonderful dirt routes along the crest. No water or services.

TIME & DISTANCE: A day. About 75 miles from Bishop via Silver Canyon and out to Big Pine on U.S. 395.

GETTING THERE: 3.8 miles north of Bishop on U.S. Highway 6, turn east onto Silver Canyon Road. To take the beautiful drive up the paved road, go south 15 miles on U.S. 395 toward Big Pine. Turn northeast on Highway 168. After 12.7 miles turn north on White Mountain Road. You can take the drive in the opposite direction if you prefer.

THE DRIVE: You'll travel on good dirt roads along the dry, rolling crest of the White Mountains, the highest range in the Great Basin. You'll see western bristlecone pines that are thousands of years old. While the steep Silver Canyon route is a fascinating geologic and scenic experience, and not difficult, it is hair-raising indeed. The drive starts at 4,140 feet in Bishop. It climbs to 11,650 feet at the trailhead to the White Mountain Research Station run by the University of California, Berkeley, an observatory and the summit of White Mountain Peak (a steep 15-mile round-trip hike).

REST STOPS: The Laws Railroad Museum 4 miles north of Bishop, off Highway 6; the Paiute Shoshone Cultural Center in Bishop, a mile west of U.S. 395 on West Line Street. Free and nice, but waterless, Grandview campground is about 5 miles north of Highway 168 on the White Mountain Road. Schulman Grove has the oldest known bristlecones; Patriarch Grove has the largest known (have lunch there). Try funky Bishop Grill ("What kin I getcha, hon?") for breakfast; Bishop's excellent Whiskey Creek for dinner. Bishop has a wonderful park. Next to it is the charming Elms Motel.

GETTING HOME: U.S. 395 north or south.

MAP: Inyo National Forest, 1993 edition. (It mistakenly shows the Silver Canyon Road as permanently closed.)

INFORMATION: White Mountain Ranger Station, Bishop, 619-873-2500.

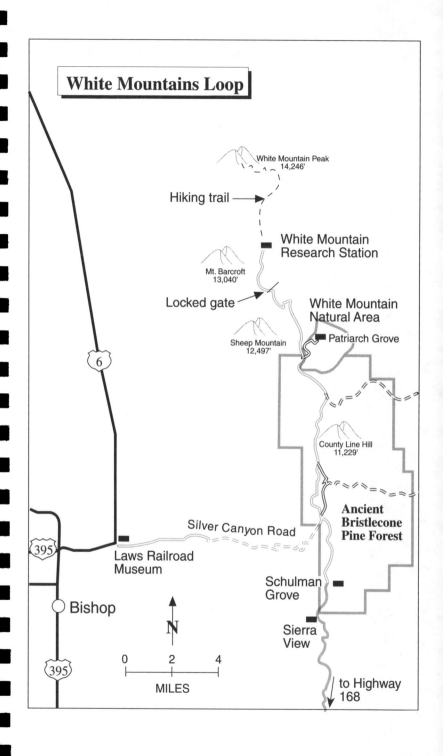

White Mountains Loop

White Mountain Peak
14,246'

Hiking trail ➞

White Mountain
Research Station

Mt. Barcroft
13,040'

Locked gate ➞

White Mountain
Natural Area

Sheep Mountain
12,497'

Patriarch Grove

County Line Hill
11,229'

**Ancient
Bristlecone
Pine Forest**

Silver Canyon Road

Laws Railroad
Museum

Schulman
Grove

Bishop

N

0   2   4
MILES

Sierra
View

to Highway
168

6

395

395

Owens Valley/Death Valley

LOCATION: Begins at Big Pine, on U.S. 395, and continues to Death Valley National Park.

HIGHLIGHTS: Largest single mountain range (Sierras) in the Lower 48; highest point (Mt. Whitney) in the contiguous states; deepest valley (Owens) in the U.S.; lowest point (Death Valley) in the Western Hemisphere; highest dunes (Eureka Dunes) in the Great Basin; Ubehebe Crater. Scotty's Castle.

DIFFICULTY: Easy, on a twisting Inyo County road that is mostly paved, except for a 31-mile stretch. Extreme heat in summer, when flash floods can close the road. Winter snow can close the section over the Inyo Mountains.

TIME & DISTANCE: 5 to 6 hours; about 110 miles to the turnoff to Scotty's Castle.

GETTING THERE: From Big Pine on U.S. 395, drive east on state Highway 168 for 2.2 miles. Turn right (southeast) onto Big Pine-Death Valley Road.

THE DRIVE: Following the paved road from Highway 168 over the Inyo Mountains, you'll pass through the narrows of Devil's Gate. From the turnoff to Saline Valley, at about 7,200 feet above sea level, the road is barely two lanes of asphalt as it winds through desert hills and descends into Little Cowhorn Valley, and then into Joshua Flats. After vast Eureka Valley appears you'll begin an ear-popping descent. To the east is the Last Chance Range. About 0.6 miles after passing North Eureka Valley Road on the left, turn south onto South Eureka Valley Road for the easy 10-mile (one way) drive to Eureka Dunes. Archaeologists have found evidence that native people gathered near the huge dunes for thousands of years. The main road will be paved through Hanging Rock Canyon. You'll see a sulfur mine and yellow outcrops on the roadside as you cross the Last Chance Range. Soon you'll reach Crankshaft Crossing, marked by old car parts, and begin the 4,000-foot plunge to Death Valley. In 21 miles you'll reach pavement.

REST STOPS: Scotty's Castle has fuel, water, shade. Eureka Dunes has primitive and waterless camping.

GETTING HOME: Via Stovepipe Wells or Furnace Creek.

MAP: BLM's Eureka-Saline Desert Access Guide.

INFORMATION: Death Valley National Park, 619-786-2331. Eastern Sierra InterAgency Visitor Center at Lone Pine, 619-876-6222.

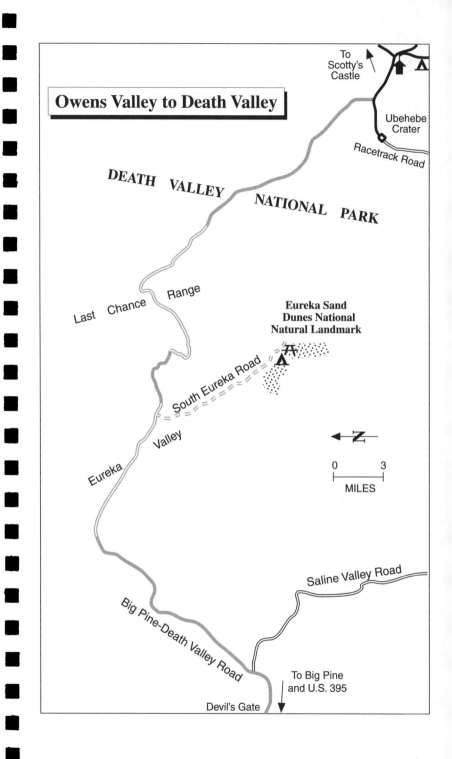

Owens Valley to Death Valley

To Scotty's Castle

Ubehebe Crater

Racetrack Road

DEATH VALLEY NATIONAL PARK

Last Chance Range

Eureka Sand Dunes National Natural Landmark

South Eureka Road

Eureka Valley

N

0   3
MILES

Saline Valley Road

Big Pine-Death Valley Road

To Big Pine and U.S. 395

Devil's Gate

Inyo Mountains

LOCATION: East of Independence and Big Pine.

HIGHLIGHTS: Superb views of the Sierra; Papoose Flat.

DIFFICULTY: Moderate. Some steep stretches with rocks and loose soil; several short side hills that require extra caution. A summer/fall drive. Requires experience. No water.

TIME & DISTANCE: All day. About 70 miles.

GETTING THERE: South of Independence turn east on Mazourka Canyon Road from U.S. 395. Set the odometer at 0.

THE DRIVE: As you near the mountains, look high and slightly north for Winnedumah, or Paiute Monument, a famous spire. At the mountains, veer left (north) on the dirt road into dramatic Mazourka Canyon. It's unusual in that it runs north-south instead of the more typical east-west. You'll pass old mines. At 12.3 miles you'll reach the left (west) turn to Santa Rita Flat, which provides a sample of what's to come. The main route will go up Al Rose Canyon. By 18.1 miles you'll reach Badger Flat. Go left. After about 1.1 mile more you'll pass a right fork you'll follow later. Keeping left, follow a track that climbs to an electronic site and an unsurpassed view of the Sierras and the Owens Valley from 9,412-foot Mazourka Peak. Return to that right fork, curving northeast past a corral. About 0.1 mile beyond Blue Bell Mine (not on the 1993 map), go left. Climb steeply up a rough stretch toward a saddle. Just after going down a dip, you'll see a small Y. Descend on the left track; 0.2 mile farther note the points of folded rock. Cross two sidehills. Descend to a small valley. Note the track to the north-west (left) from the valley floor; that's the route you'll take. But once in the bowl, climb to the right toward a crest and the ridge overlooking Waucoba Canyon, Side Hill Spring and the vast desert to the east. Return to the valley; go west. After 2.3 miles the road seems to vanish, but it's to the left. Carefully descend to a flat with campsites; turn right down to Papoose Flat. Go north on road 9S15 toward views of the White Mountains and desert valleys below. You'll descend on tortuous switchbacks, and come out on Saline Valley/Eureka Valley Road. Big Pine is left (west).

REST STOPS: Camp at Badger Flat. Visit the site of the old Manzanar internment camp; Eastern California Museum.

GETTING HOME: U.S. 395 north or south.

MAP: Inyo National Forest, 1993 edition.

INFORMATION: Mt. Whitney Ranger Station, 619-876-6200.

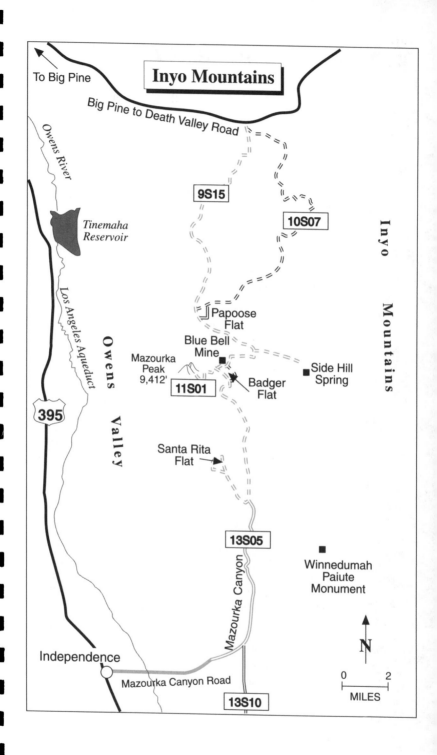

Inyo Mountains

To Big Pine

Big Pine to Death Valley Road

Owens River

Tinemaha Reservoir

Los Angeles Aqueduct

Owens Valley

395

9S15

10S07

Inyo Mountains

Papoose Flat

Blue Bell Mine

Mazourka Peak 9,412'

11S01

Badger Flat

Side Hill Spring

Santa Rita Flat

13S05

Winnedumah Paiute Monument

Mazourka Canyon

Independence

Mazourka Canyon Road

13S10

N

0   2
MILES

Saline Valley Road

LOCATION: Between Owens Valley & Death Valley.

HIGHLIGHTS: Contrast between the snowy high Sierras and desert basin and range country; hot springs. Vista of Panamint Valley. Historic sites. Very remote.

DIFFICULTY: Easy; badly washboarded. North and South passes can be closed in winter. Flash floods can close the road at times in summer. Very hot in summer. No services.

TIME & DISTANCE: 5 to 6 hours. About 100 miles from Big Pine on U.S. 395 to state Highway 190.

GETTING THERE: From Big Pine on U.S. 395, take Highway 168 east for 2.2 miles. Go right on the Big Pine-Death Valley Road, a.k.a. Saline Valley/Eureka Valley Road. 13.1 miles later Waucoba/Saline Valley Road branches southeast; set your odometer at 0.

THE DRIVE: Inhospitable as Saline Valley seems, its marsh supports plant and animal life, and archaeologists have found evidence of human habitation going back at least 10,000 years. Drive through the narrows of Devil's Gate on the paved road to Death Valley (described separately). Where the Saline Valley Road turns southeast, you're at about 7,500 feet above sea level. After 14.5 miles you'll see a forbidding trough in the distance, Saline Valley, surrounded by huge mountains. East of the road is Death Valley National Park. You'll drop fast, passing through washes that suggest the power of flash floods. At 32.4 miles you may see a painted rock on the left, at the entrance to a road to developed hot springs. (Clothing optional.) The valley floor is about 1,100 feet above sea level. (By now you've noticed how severely washboarded the road has become.) The ruins of salt works and a tram, built between 1911-1913 to transport salt over the Inyo Mountains, can be seen about 2 miles south of the marsh. Ignore the dicey 4x4 trail to Lippincott Mine. By 58 miles you'll enter Grapevine Canyon, with wild vines, willows and Joshua trees. You'll reach the Panamint Valley vista. It's 17 miles to Highway 190.

REST STOPS: Soaking, primitive camping at Lower Warm Spring and Palm Spring. Panamint Springs, on Hwy. 190.

GETTING HOME: Highway 190 east to Death Valley or west to U.S. 395, 39 miles from Saline Valley Road.

MAP: BLM's Eureka-Saline Desert Access Guide.

INFORMATION: BLM, Ridgecrest, 619-375-7125; Death Valley National Park, 619-786-2331; Eastern Sierra InterAgency Visitor Center, 619-876-6222.

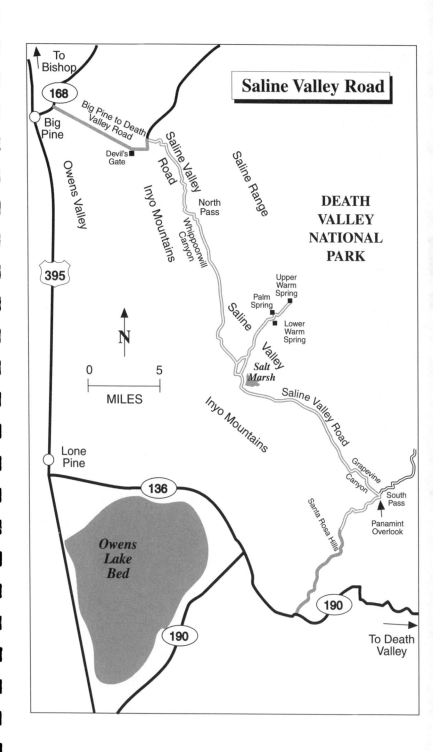

Saline Valley Road

The Racetrack

LOCATION: Northern Death Valley National Park.

HIGHLIGHTS: Ubehebe Crater; Joshua trees; dry lakebed called The Racetrack and its moving rocks. Hidden Valley.

DIFFICULTY: Easy, but you'll endure some rocky driving. It can get snow in winter, and may have muddy spots.

TIME & DISTANCE: A full day. About 55 miles round-trip from Ubehebe Crater.

GETTING THERE: Drive to Ubehebe Crater. The road begins just beyond it.

THE DRIVE: Ubehebe Crater is an explosion pit caused when water came into contact with molten rock that worked its way up through fissures caused by the Death Valley fault zone. The blast created a crater a half-mile wide and 750 feet deep. Driving between the Cottonwood Mountains to the south and the Last Chance Range to the north, the rocky road will give you an idea of how much rock has eroded down from the mountains. Notice the variety of cacti along the way. You'll climb from about 2,400 feet above sea level at the start to almost 5,000 feet at Tin Pass, then descend to about 4,000 feet at The Racetrack. About 20 miles from the crater you'll pass through Teakettle Junction. A good side trip is to turn left (south) and go up the wash through narrow Lost Burro Gap to Hidden Valley and Ulida Flat (described separately). The Racetrack is 6 miles beyond Teakettle Junction. Do not drive on the playa (a usually dry lakebed). Walk out to the neat "Grandstand," the tip of a mountain that was buried by eroding material from the surrounding mountains. There is a parking area at the south end of The Racetrack. From there you can search the playa for the moving rocks. It's unclear why rocks slide, unseen, across the lakebed. One theory is that wind pushes them when precipitation makes the playa slick.

REST STOPS: There's a battered outhouse at Lippincott Mine, 1.6 miles beyond The Racetrack. It's a lousy place to camp, even though some maps show a camping area there.

GETTING HOME: Return the way you came in. Or, if time and road conditions permit, go through Hidden Valley and over Hunter Mountain to Saline Valley Road. The 4x4 trail down from Lippincott Mine to Saline Valley Road is very rough.

MAP: BLM's Eureka-Saline Desert Access Guide, or Trails Illustrated's Death Valley topographic map.

INFORMATION: The Furnace Creek Visitor Center, or call the park at 619-786-2331.

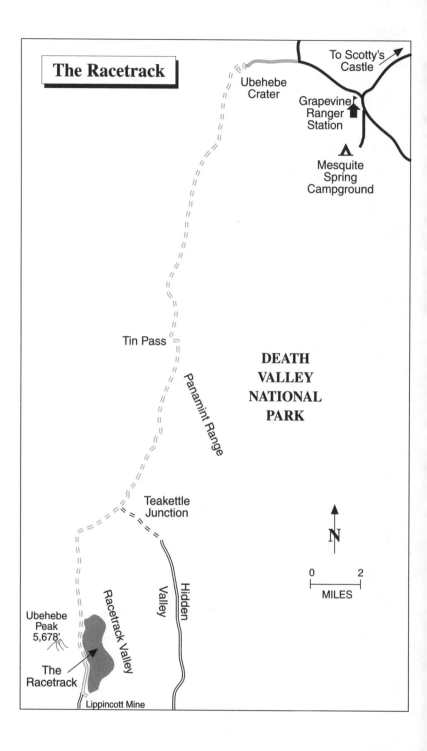

The Racetrack

To Scotty's Castle

Ubehebe Crater

Grapevine Ranger Station

Mesquite Spring Campground

Tin Pass

Panamint Range

DEATH VALLEY NATIONAL PARK

Teakettle Junction

N

0   2
MILES

Ubehebe Peak 5,678'

Racetrack Valley

Hidden Valley

The Racetrack

Lippincott Mine

Cerro Gordo

LOCATION: Inyo Mountains, east of Lone Pine.

HIGHLIGHTS: Ghost town (private property); beautiful canyons and sweeping vistas as you climb almost 8 miles up a narrow road from 3,700 feet elevation in the Owens Valley to more than 8,000 feet. A gorgeous descent to Death Valley National Park.

DIFFICULTY: Easy, though the climb is steep on a narrow dirt and gravel road. Descent is a bit rocky. The road is subject to washouts. Snow can block it in winter.

TIME & DISTANCE: 2.5 hours; 33 miles from the start of Cerro Gordo Road over the mountains to Highway 190.

GETTING THERE: From U.S. 395 south of Lone Pine, take state Highway 136 southeast to Keeler. Turn northeast onto Cerro Gordo Road; set your odometer at 0.

THE DRIVE: Cerro Gordo (Spanish for "Fat Hill") is the name of the nearby 9,184-foot peak, the fairly well-preserved and authentic 19th century ghost town, and the mines that produced many millions of dollars worth of silver, lead and zinc. Silver was discovered here in 1865. By 1871, the town had nearly 2,000 people. The silver boom ended by 1879, but in the early 1900s Cerro Gordo became the nation's foremost producer of high-grade zinc. The mines continued producing ore intermittently until 1936. Drive across the alluvial fan into a fascinating canyon. As you climb steeply you'll get outstanding vistas of the Owens Valley and Sierras. At Cerro Gordo you'll see a number of relatively well-preserved buildings. The ghost town is the most intensively posted private property I've ever seen. Only through traffic is allowed on the road, maintained by Inyo County. Drive through the town to a scenic crest. From there you'll descend to San Lucas Canyon, turning right (southeast) at 12.9 miles at a T intersection. You'll soon be driving along the western boundary of Death Valley National Park. At 17.5 miles keep left. Cross Lee Flat, and pass through a Joshua tree forest. At 24.5 miles you'll reach Saline Valley Road. Go right to Highway 190.

REST STOPS: Lone Pine has all services, including a great park. Food, water, fuel, lodging at Panamint Springs.

GETTING HOME: Via Death Valley or U.S. 395.

MAPS: BLM's Eureka-Saline, Panamint Desert Guides.

INFORMATION: Eastern Sierra InterAgency Visitor Center at Lone Pine, 619-876-6222.

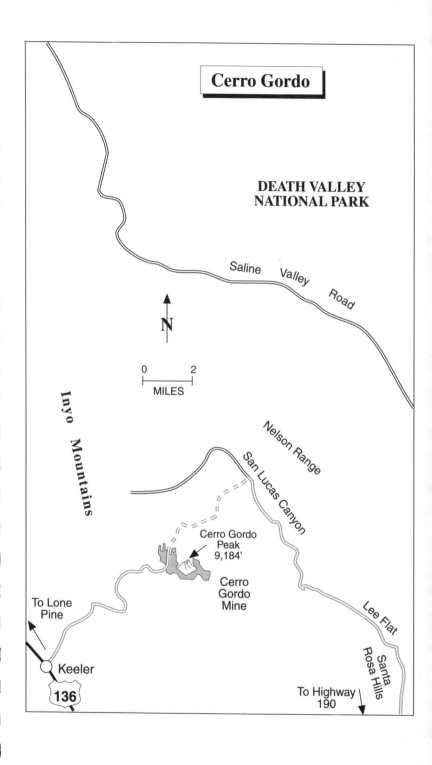

Cerro Gordo

DEATH VALLEY NATIONAL PARK

Saline Valley Road

N

0   2
MILES

Inyo Mountains

Nelson Range

San Lucas Canyon

Cerro Gordo Peak
9,184'

Cerro Gordo Mine

Lee Flat

Santa Rosa Hills

To Lone Pine

Keeler

136

To Highway 190

Hidden Valley

LOCATION: East of Racetrack Valley in Death Valley National Park, in the Cottonwood Mountains.

HIGHLIGHTS: A broad valley at about 5,000 feet elevation that is cooler than Death Valley; limestone narrows of Lost Burro Gap; The Racetrack; Joshua trees; great vistas.

DIFFICULTY: Easy. Hunter Mountain segment may be closed in winter by ice and snow. Check ahead.

TIME & DISTANCE: All day. If you approach from Ubehebe Crater via Racetrack Road, you'll drive about 80 miles round-trip. From Saline Valley Road over Hunter Mountain to Teakettle Junction is about 25 miles.

GETTING THERE: South from Racetrack Road at Teakettle Junction, or northeast off Saline Valley Road at South Pass.

THE DRIVE: See the descriptions for the drives to The Racetrack and Saline Valley. From Racetrack Road, turn south at Teakettle Junction. Drive up a gravel wash between the narrow cliffs of Lost Burro Gap. Just after the gap, a road goes northeast toward White Top Mountain, past two springs you can hike to. The road gets steep, but you can drive to about a quarter-mile from White Top and hike the rest of the way for a spectacular view of Death Valley below. Continue south through Hidden Valley to Ulida Flat and the Joshua tree forest, and a mining area. Climb up toward Hunter Mountain on the one-lane, sometimes rocky road. Almost 7 miles from Ulida Flat, near the old monument boundary, a road branches off to the north (right) for several miles, climbing to about 6,500 feet through Joshua trees to a great vista of Hidden Valley and Racetrack Valley. If you're starting from Saline Valley Road, you'll climb over relatively lush Hunter Mountain from about 6,200 feet at South Pass to about 7,000 feet through pinyon trees and juniper. The vista road near the old monument boundary goes left from the Hunter Mountain Road about 7 miles from Saline Valley Road.

REST STOPS: The Racetrack; Hunter Mountain.

GETTING HOME: Return the way you came. Or go south about 17 miles from South Pass on Saline Valley Road to state Highway 190. Or drive to the pavement at Ubehebe Crater. The road from Lippincott Mine, southwest of The Racetrack, to Saline Valley is dangerous. Skip it.

MAP: BLM's Eureka-Saline Desert Access Guide, or Trails Illustrated's Death Valley topographic map.

INFORMATION: Death Valley N.P., 619-786-2331.

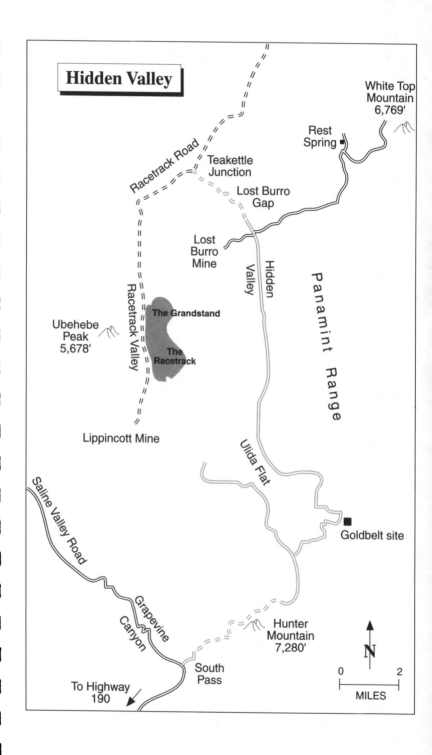

Hidden Valley

White Top Mountain 6,769'

Rest Spring

Racetrack Road

Teakettle Junction

Lost Burro Gap

Lost Burro Mine

Hidden Valley

Panamint Range

Racetrack Valley

The Grandstand

Ubehebe Peak 5,678'

The Racetrack

Lippincott Mine

Ulida Flat

Goldbelt site

Saline Valley Road

Grapevine Canyon

Hunter Mountain 7,280'

South Pass

To Highway 190

N

0   2

MILES

Titus Canyon

LOCATION: Grapevine Mountains; northeastern Death Valley National Park.

HIGHLIGHTS: One of the park's most beautiful drives. Ghost town of Rhyolite; ruins at Leadfield; a narrow, high-walled canyon slicing through the Grapevines' western slope; petroglyphs and possible desert bighorn sheep at Klare Spring.

DIFFICULTY: Easy. Can only be driven east to west. Closed May to October to give the bighorn undisturbed access to Klare Spring. The narrow dirt road is often washed out by floods. Get road conditions at the Furnace Creek visitor center.

TIME & DISTANCE: Half a day to appreciate the place. About 27 miles.

GETTING THERE: Take Hwy. 374 toward Beatty, Nev.

THE DRIVE: Visit the nearby ghost town of Rhyolite. The Titus Canyon road begins off Highway 374 about 7 miles east of the California/Nevada state line. It will take you from the Amargosa Desert up some switchbacks to Red Pass, at about 4,200 feet above sea level, through the Grapevine Mountains to about 165 feet above sea level at Death Valley. You'll pass through multicolored volcanic stream, lakebed and ocean deposits. You'll pass the site of Leadfield, a short-lived mining town founded in 1925 by C.C. Julian, the largest investor. Much money was spent on holes that missed the ore. When they found it, bad luck continued when the engine for the mill failed to arrive. After further mishaps, Julian lost his fortune, and other investors blamed him for their losses. Narrow, high-walled Titus Canyon is beyond Leadfield and Klare Spring. It was named in 1906 for a young mining engineer, Morris Titus, who disappeared in the canyon when searching for water. Drive ends at Highway 190.

REST STOPS: A number of places along the way, including Leadfield, where you'll find old mines. Services at Beatty, Scotty's Castle or Stovepipe Wells.

GETTING HOME: South toward Stovepipe Wells, Furnace Creek and state Highway 190.

MAPS: Trails Illustrated's Death Valley topographic map and the park brochure.

INFORMATION: Death Valley National Park, 619-786-2331. Bring a copy of Roger Brandt's "Titus Canyon Road Guide."

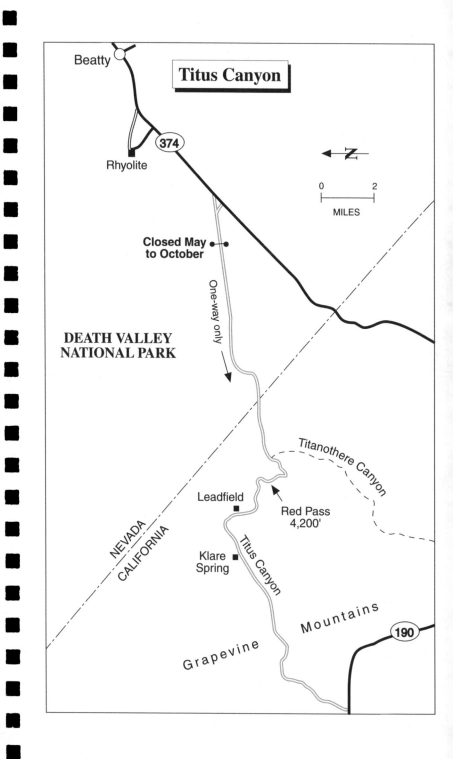

Titus Canyon

Beatty

Rhyolite

374

N

0   2
MILES

Closed May to October

One-way only

DEATH VALLEY NATIONAL PARK

Titanothere Canyon

Leadfield

Red Pass 4,200'

NEVADA
CALIFORNIA

Klare Spring

Titus Canyon

Mountains

190

Grapevine

Chloride City

LOCATION: Southwest of Beatty, Nev., near the eastern boundary of Death Valley National Park.

HIGHLIGHTS: Spectacular view of Death Valley and the Sierras to the west; the ghost town of Chloride City and its associated mines.

DIFFICULTY: Easy if you take the eastern route (described below) round-trip. Moderate if you exit on the scenic western route to Boundary Canyon, about midway between Daylight Pass and Hell's Gate on Hwy. 374.

TIME & DISTANCE: 5 hours; 28 miles round-trip. There are many roads to explore that can add up to 6 miles.

GETTING THERE: Go toward Beatty on Highway 374 to the park boundary. Turn right (south) on the dirt road just outside the park.

THE DRIVE: You'll start at an elevation of about 3,400 feet and climb to Chloride Cliff at about 5,400 feet. The road is easy but sections can wash out in heavy rains. Vegetation for the first 11 miles is predominantly creosote bush, but you'll also see sage, box thorn and desert trumpet. The rocks early in the drive are mostly ash deposits from volcanic centers to the east. Rock types change around mile 9.8 to ocean deposits of sand and mud. These deposits are among the oldest rocks in the park at about 800 million years old. At mile 11 go left and continue on to Chloride City. You'll reach a view of Chloride City at mile 12.2. This was Death Valley's first mining claim, established in 1871. The structures were built after 1903 when this entire region experienced a silver and lead mining boom. Chloride Cliff is another mile ahead beyond the saddle on the other side of the town site. To reach the saddle keep left at the forks. Go left again when you get to the saddle. Follow the road from here to the obvious high point. Walk the last 50 feet to the top of Chloride Cliff. Remember, park rules prohibit collecting or removing anything.

REST STOPS: Chloride Cliff and Chloride City site.

GETTING HOME: Retrace your route, or take the rougher 4x4 route to Highway 374 in Boundary Canyon. To do the latter, return to mile 11 and turn west at the fork. After half a mile the road forks again. Left goes to other mines, right to the highway in about 9 miles.

MAPS: BLM's Amargosa Desert Access Guide, or Trails Illustrated's Death Valley topographic map.

INFORMATION: Death Valley N.P., 619-786-2331.

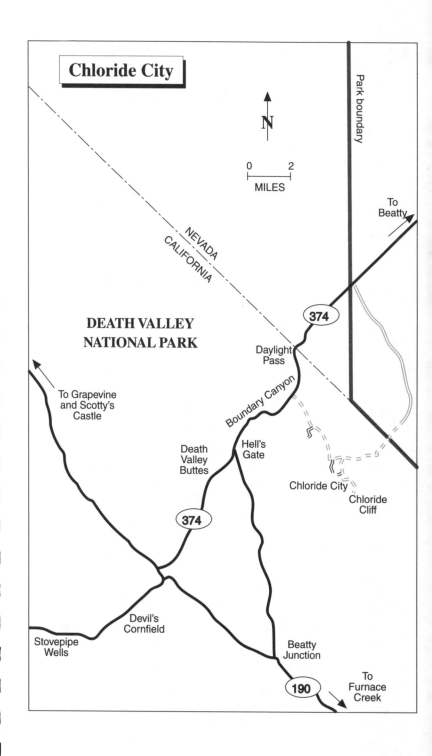

Chloride City

N

0 — 2
MILES

To Beatty

Park boundary

NEVADA
CALIFORNIA

DEATH VALLEY
NATIONAL PARK

374

Daylight
Pass

Boundary Canyon

To Grapevine
and Scotty's
Castle

Death
Valley
Buttes

Hell's
Gate

Chloride City

Chloride
Cliff

374

Devil's
Cornfield

Stovepipe
Wells

Beatty
Junction

To
Furnace
Creek

190

Cottonwood/Marble canyons

LOCATION: In the Cottonwood Mountains west of Stovepipe Wells in Death Valley National Park.

HIGHLIGHTS: Limestone narrows of Marble Canyon; petroglyphs; Cottonwood Springs. You'll climb from sea level to about 3,500 feet elevation.

DIFFICULTY: Moderate. Some maneuvering between rocks; a patch of sand at mile 17 in Cottonwood Canyon.

TIME & DISTANCE: All day. Round-trip distance for Cottonwood Canyon is 38 miles. Marble Canyon adds another 8 miles.

GETTING THERE: The road starts off Highway 190 about 100 feet west of the store in Stovepipe Wells. This also is used as the campground entrance. Set your odometer at 0 where the road begins at Highway 190.

THE DRIVE: Go about 100 feet and turn left on the road marked "airstrip." The road is paved for the next half mile. Keep right at the fork where the pavement ends. The road crosses the valley and climbs onto a bench where desert pavement can be seen. A good vista point is located at mile 8.7 just before you drop into Cottonwood Wash. Camping is allowed from this point on. Logs and branches of wood in this wash come from Cottonwood Springs, where a grove of cottonwood trees are located. It is against park rules to collect this wood for fires. Unusual "balls" of black chert, a rock made of millions of microscopic organisms called radiolarians, can be seen in the gray limestone outcrop at mile 9.6. These rocks were formed 400 million years ago in an ancient sea. Petroglyphs are located on the cliff to the left at mile 9.7. Many of the etchings found here were made in recent years by vandals. Recent etchings are white, compared to the dull gray of the weathered petroglyphs made 6,000 years ago. You will need to maneuver between boulders for the next half mile. At mile 11, the road to Marble Canyon goes right and dead ends after 3.8 miles. Large vehicles will not be able to pass a narrow notch at mile 2.7. The narrow canyon is a beautiful place to walk. The Cottonwood Canyon road (straight ahead at mile 11) dead ends at mile 19. You'll see granite outcrops and running water from springs.

REST STOPS: Vista point; Cottonwood Springs.

GETTING HOME: Return to Stovepipe Wells.

MAP: Trails Illustrated's map of Death Valley.

INFORMATION: Death Valley N.P., 619-786-2331.

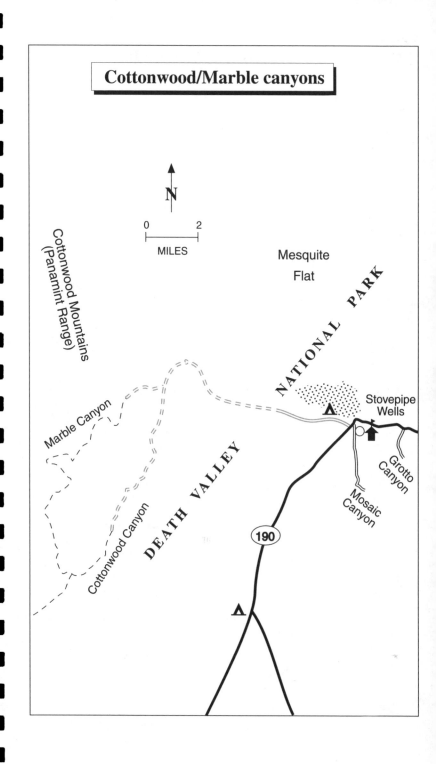

Cottonwood/Marble canyons

N

0   2
MILES

Cottonwood Mountains
(Panamint Range)

Mesquite
Flat

NATIONAL PARK

Marble Canyon

Stovepipe
Wells

DEATH VALLEY

Cottonwood Canyon

Grotto
Canyon

Mosaic
Canyon

190

Echo Canyon

LOCATION: Death Valley National Park, east of Furnace Creek in the Funeral Mountains.

HIGHLIGHTS: High-walled canyon; Eye of the Needle; historic Inyo Mine; 3,000-foot elevation gain; convenient.

DIFFICULTY: Easy. There's a short rock outcrop to cross.

TIME & DISTANCE: 4-5 hours; 18.8 miles round-trip.

GETTING THERE: From Furnace Creek, take state Hwy. 190 southeast. About 2 miles beyond the junction with Highway 178, turn left at the sign for Echo Canyon.

THE DRIVE: You'll start out at about 400 feet above sea level, and climb to about 3,500 feet. For the first 3 miles you'll drive across an alluvial fan. Ahead, you'll see the chocolate-colored mountains and canyon walls of 500 million-year-old limestone and mud sediments from the Cambrian geologic period. The first shelled fossils appear in the old sea bed and ocean deposits from this period. Just as you enter the canyon, you'll reach a tricky rock outcrop. You might find the left approach easiest. As you drive, you'll witness the simultaneous geologic action of uplifting, folding and erosion. By 4.7 miles, look up and to your right to see the eroded window, Eye of the Needle. By 5.2 miles you'll enter a bowl where you can see dramatic geology. You'll pass through some narrows. At mile 7.7 keep right at the fork. At about 8.6 miles you'll pass through an open area that is the site of Schwaub, but there's nothing left to see of the camp that sprouted after gold was discovered in the canyon in 1905. Avoid the rough road that branches left at about 8.9 miles. By about 9.4 miles you'll reach the ruins of Inyo Mine, one of Death Valley's most historic sites. Inadequate financing and lack of water for milling doomed attempts to fully exploit the gold reserves. It was last worked in 1940. Note: Old mines and their buildings are dangerous. It's illegal to collect or remove objects from national parks.

REST STOPS: Inyo Mine. No camping is allowed for the first 4 miles. Services are available at Furnace Creek.

ALSO TRY: The 2.7-mile drive through Twenty Mule Team Canyon, about 2.5 miles south of the Echo Canyon turnoff; nearby Hole-In-The-Wall Road, Trip No. 13.

MAPS: BLM's Amargosa Desert Access Guide, or Trails Illustrated's Death Valley topographic map.

INFORMATION: Death Valley N.P., 619-786-2331; visitor center at Furnace Creek.

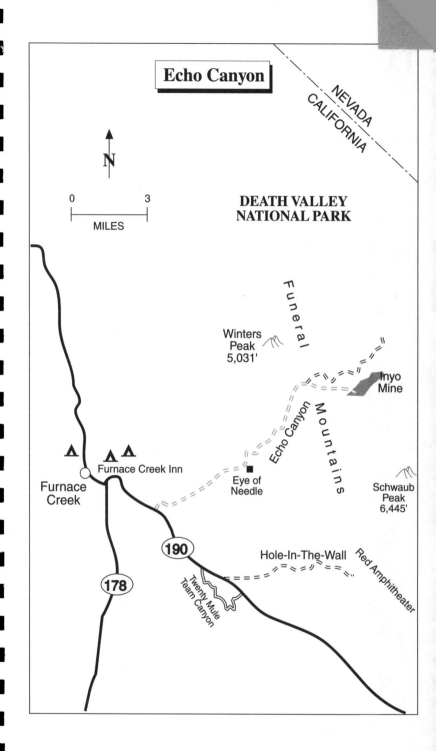

Echo Canyon

N

0   3
MILES

DEATH VALLEY NATIONAL PARK

NEVADA
CALIFORNIA

Funeral

Mountains

Winters Peak
5,031'

Inyo Mine

Echo Canyon

Furnace Creek Inn

Eye of Needle

Schwaub Peak
6,445'

Furnace Creek

190

Hole-In-The-Wall

Red Amphitheater

178

Twenty Mule Team Canyon

Hole-In-The-Wall

LOCATION: Death Valley National Park, southeast of Furnace Creek in the Funeral Mountains.

HIGHLIGHTS: Hole-In-The-Wall; Schwaub Peak.

DIFFICULTY: Easy to moderate. Patches of soft gravel.

TIME & DISTANCE: An hour if you only take the 8-mile round trip to Hole-In-The-Wall; 4 hours if you take the 18-mile round-trip to the upper part of the wash.

GETTING THERE: From the Furnace Creek Visitor Center, take state Highway 190 southeast for 6.8 miles. The route is in a wash near the 1,000-foot elevation marker along the highway, about midway between the entrance and exit for Twenty-Mule Team Canyon. Set your odometer at 0.

THE DRIVE: The road winds through stands of creosote bush and pygmy cedar for the first 3 miles. The driving is easy on a solid gravel base. Tan-colored sediments from a lake that existed 6 million years ago become visible at mile 1.2 and continue for the next 2.5 miles. Ripple marks can be seen in some locations. Hole-In-The-Wall is located at mile 3.9. The site is named for the ridge of sediments that were pushed into a vertical position by the Furnace Creek fault, which is no longer active. The complete ridge or "wall" can be seen better from the east side. From here, hundreds of small, cavernous openings can be seen covering the wall. The roadbed gravel becomes looser and deeper for the next mile. Cactus can be seen along this stretch. Prospecting sites are marked by roads that go off to the right and left at mile 6.3. Neither go far. At mile 7.4 you will see the spectacular striped slopes of Schwaub Peak ahead in the distance. Pyramid Peak is to the right. Both mountains are made of sediments from a shallow, tropical ocean that covered this area about 400 million years ago. The rock outcrop on the left at mile 8.1 will give you a close look at these rocks. The orange-hued streaks are chert, a rock made of microscopic organisms called radiolarians. The dark–colored rock is limestone. Remember, no collecting or removal of rocks is allowed in any national park. At mile 9 the road takes a sharp left and goes up a steep wash with many areas of deep sand and gravel. Don't go any farther.

REST STOPS: Hole-In-The-Wall; walk the prospector's roads at mile 6.3.

GETTING HOME: Return to Highway 190.

MAP: Trails Illustrated's map of Death Valley.

INFORMATION: Death Valley N.P., 619-786-2331.

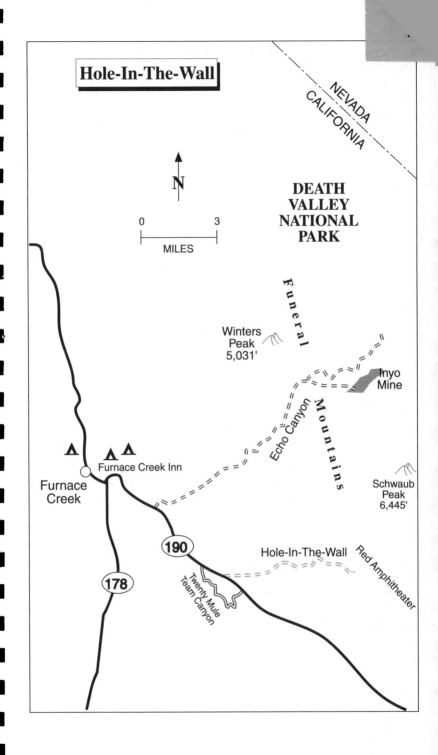

Hole-In-The-Wall

NEVADA
CALIFORNIA

DEATH
VALLEY
NATIONAL
PARK

N

0   3
MILES

Winters
Peak
5,031'

Funeral

Inyo
Mine

Echo Canyon

Mountains

Schwaub
Peak
6,445'

Furnace Creek Inn

Furnace
Creek

190

Hole-In-The-Wall   Red Amphitheater

178

Twenty Mule
Team Canyon

Darwin Falls to Darwin

LOCATION: Death Valley National Park south of state Highway 190 and southwest of Panamint Springs.

HIGHLIGHTS: Hiking up to Darwin Falls, a rare year-round 30-foot desert waterfall and stream; stratified rock of Darwin Canyon; old mining town of Darwin; views of Panamint Valley.

DIFFICULTY: Easy; one short, moderate 4x4 pitch. A half-mile hike to the falls; easiest in fall and winter; hot and humid in summer. Carry water.

TIME & DISTANCE: 2 to 3 hours; about 19 miles.

GETTING THERE: 1 mile west of Panamint Springs, or about 44 miles east of U.S. 395, turn south onto Darwin Canyon Road. Set your odometer at 0 and cross Darwin Wash. At 2.4 miles turn right at the sign for the falls, and drive up the wash into a canyon until you reach a barricade and parking area.

THE DRIVE: After visiting the falls, return to Darwin Canyon, and 1.5 miles later you'll go up a short rocky stretch (use low range). Go over a summit (about 3,600 feet) and in another 0.7 miles you'll be in a wide wash at the base of stratified canyon walls. Continue along the base of the canyon, and you'll soon reach oiled gravel. You'll pass Joshua trees, and then come to Darwin. It was named after Darwin French, who explored the area in 1860. Lead and silver were found in the hills here in 1875. Darwin became the center of activity in the New Coso Mining District, where gold, zinc and copper were also mined. Today it's a silent quasi-ghost town that feels something like an Australian outback settlement. Go right at the old Post Office and gas station with the two old pumps. About 6.5 paved miles later you'll be at Highway 190.

REST STOPS: Stock up on refreshments and fuel at Panamint Springs Resort, where there's a store and restaurant.

GETTING HOME: Highway 190 west to Olancha and U.S. 395, or east to Death Valley.

MAP: BLM's Panamint Desert Access Guide.

INFORMATION: Death Valley National Park, 619-786-2331; Eastern Sierra InterAgency Visitor Center at Lone Pine, 619-876-6222.

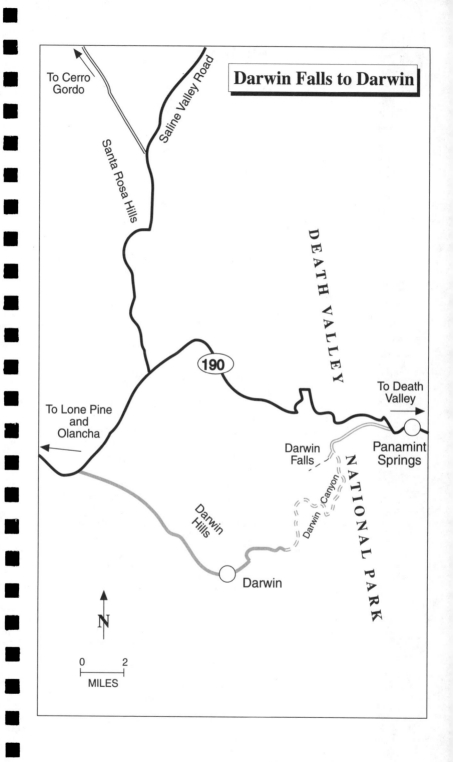

Darwin Falls to Darwin

To Cerro Gordo

Saline Valley Road

Santa Rosa Hills

DEATH VALLEY

190

To Death Valley

To Lone Pine and Olancha

Darwin Falls

Panamint Springs

Darwin Hills

Darwin Canyon

NATIONAL PARK

Darwin

N

0   2
MILES

Butte Valley

LOCATION: Panamint Range, southern Death Valley N.P.

HIGHLIGHTS: A high and beautiful valley. Old miners' cabins you can stay in (some with water and furniture), including the hideout of murderer Charles Manson and his "family." High-walled Goler Wash is fascinating. You'll climb from about −165 feet to 4,326 feet at Mengel Pass. Wildflowers late April to mid-May.

DIFFICULTY: The 14 miles from Badwater Road to White Point Mine are easy but rocky. Then it's moderate to Butte Valley. Moderate to difficult from Butte Valley to the mouth of Goler Wash. Easy to Ballarat. Flash flood danger. Winter snow is possible.

TIME & DISTANCE: 4-5 hours; 55 miles.

GETTING THERE: Take Badwater Road 42.2 miles south from Hwy. 190; go west (right) on dirt and gravel West Side Road. Or take Hwy. 178 west from Hwy. 127 near Shoshone; 30 miles from Hwy. 127, or 3.8 miles after the road bends north and becomes Badwater Road, go west (left) onto West Side Road.

THE DRIVE: From Badwater Road cross the wash of the Amargosa River, in a valley that once lay beneath ice-age Lake Manly. At mile 2.9 go left onto Butte Valley Road, which climbs through Warm Springs Canyon past billion-year-old ocean sediments. Death Valley got its name when, in the winter of 1849, several pioneer families became lost. After help arrived, they made their way to this canyon, where a pioneer turned and said, "Good-bye, death valley." Once in the canyon you'll pass some defunct talc mines, including White Point Mine at about mile 14. The bars over the tunnel opening keep people out while letting bats enter and leave. You'll soon see an old stamp mill on the left, a relic of gold mining farther up the canyon that dates as far back as the 1870s. The road is rougher from White Point Mine. By 18.2 you're out of the canyon. The road improves as you enter Butte Valley (el. 3,500 ft.). Ahead rise the upturned ocean sediments of Striped Butte. West of it is 7,196-ft. Manly Peak. Watch for wild burros. Soon you'll see so-called Geologist's Cabin, built in 1930. Anvil Spring is nearby. Past Striped Butte a road veers right. To reach a ridge with a vista and camp spot, take this spur a short way, then take one of the roads that go left up the ridge. Butte Valley Road continues past Greater View Spring and two more cabins, Stella's Place and Russell Camp. The rough road crosses Mengel Pass. In another 2.6 miles it drops left into Goler Wash. Soon you'll see willows at Sourdough Spring, where a brushy track goes left up a side canyon half a mile to the Barker Ranch and Manson's old school bus. 0.25-mile farther is the Meyers Ranch cabin. Manson was arrested at Barker Ranch on Oct. 12, 1969, for highly publicized murders in the Los Angeles area. Continue to Panamint Valley, where the good road goes north past a gold mine. To get to Trona-Wildrose Road, go left at what's left of Ballarat, an 1890s gold mining town.

REST STOPS: The cabins, maintained by users, are free; no reservations. No camping for the first 10 miles. Primitive camping is OK thereafter. Inquire about park campfire regulations.

GETTING HOME: Trona-Wildrose Road north to Hwy. 190 or south toward Ridgecrest and U.S. 395.

MAP: ACSC's *Guide to Death Valley.*

INFORMATION: Call the park at 619-786-2331.

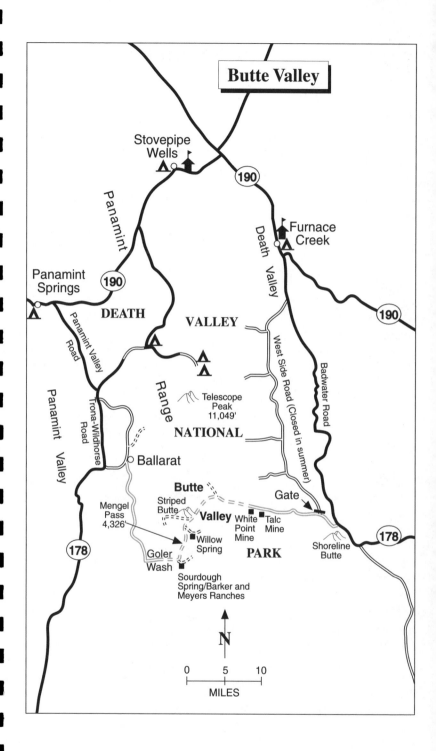

Butte Valley

Stovepipe Wells

190

Furnace Creek

Death Valley

190

Panamint Springs

190

DEATH

VALLEY

190

Panamint

Range

West Side Road (Closed in summer)

Badwater Road

Telescope Peak 11,049'

NATIONAL

Panamint Valley Road

Trona-Wildhorse Road

Ballarat

Butte

Gate

Mengel Pass 4,326'

Striped Butte

Valley

White Point Mine

Talc Mine

Panamint Valley

Willow Spring

PARK

Shoreline Butte

178

Goler Wash

178

Sourdough Spring/Barker and Meyers Ranches

N

0   5   10

MILES

Trona Pinnacles

LOCATION: About 16 miles east of Ridgecrest.

HIGHLIGHTS: One of the most outstanding collections of tufa towers (calcium carbonate deposits) in the United States. You may even get to watch a sci-fi film being made.

DIFFICULTY: Easy.

TIME & DISTANCE: 1 to 2 hours; 11 miles.

GETTING THERE: From Ridgecrest, take state Highway 178 (Trona Road) northeast for 16.6 miles. The turnoff is well-marked. You can see the tufa towers from the highway, rising like sawteeth from the gently sloping expanse of Searles Valley.

THE DRIVE: This national natural landmark has more than 500 towers, some as high as 140 feet, rising from the bed of the Searles Dry Lake basin. Their size easily eclipses the famous tufa towers at Mono Lake. They developed between 10,000 and 100,000 years ago when ancient Searles Lake formed a link in a chain of interconnected lakes fed by regular rainfall and runoff from the retreating glaciers of the Sierra Nevada Mountains. At peak periods the lake reached depths of 640 feet and overflowed into Panamint Valley and Death Valley. Its shoreline is still visible as horizontal banding on the hillsides northwest of the pinnacles. The pinnacles were formed underwater by the interaction of blue-green algae and local chemical and geothermal conditions. Hot springs welled up through fault line fractures to introduce calcium-rich ground water that combined with carbonates and formed calcium carbonate deposits. Algae bonded with the deposits, creating the pinnacle formations. When the lake dried up, the spires remained. You'll cross the dried mud at the southern end of lakebed, following road RM 143. If the lakebed is wet and muddy, don't attempt to cross it. There are great photo opportunities in this odd landscape, which is why makers of post-apocalypse films use this setting.

REST STOPS: This is a great place to let the kids romp. At Ridgecrest, visit the Maturango Museum to learn more about the cultural and natural history of the upper Mojave Desert.

GETTING HOME: Highway 178 to Ridgecrest and U.S. 395. Or continue north to Panamint and Death valleys.

MAP: BLM's Ridgecrest Desert Access Guide.

INFORMATION: BLM, Ridgecrest, 619-384-5400.

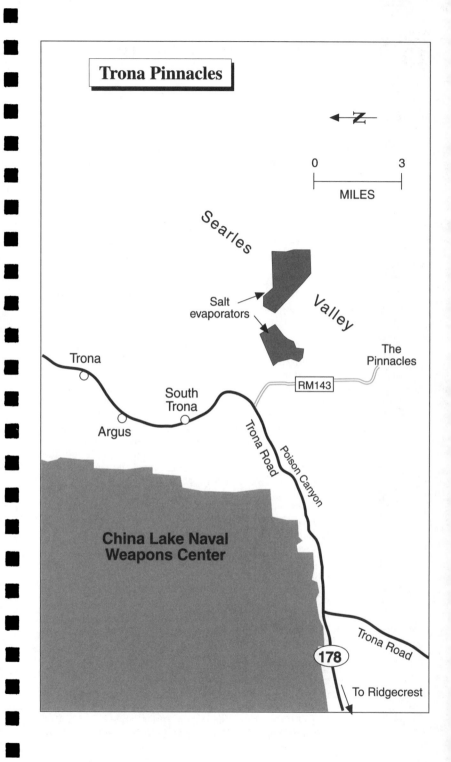

Burro Schmidt's Tunnel

LOCATION: El Paso Mountains in Kern County, east of state Highway 14 and north of the Red Rock-Randsburg Road.

HIGHLIGHTS: A hand-dug tunnel 2,087 feet long through a mountain; its owner, Tonie Seger, and her old cabins; Last Chance Canyon, rich in archaeological sites, now part of Red Rock Canyon State Park.

DIFFICULTY: Easy.

TIME & DISTANCE: 2.5 hours at least, depending on how much you explore the area. Be prepared to visit with the talkative and interesting Mrs. Seger. About 15 miles.

GETTING THERE: From Highway 14, take Red Rock-Randsburg Road northeast for 11 miles. Then, on the left, you'll see a 50-gallon drum bearing the words "Burro Schmidt Tunnel" in faded paint. Turn left; set your odometer at 0.

THE DRIVE: Go up a dirt and gravel road through a canyon into mountains that are honeycombed with old mines. Many types of minerals, metals and gems were sought up here, including copper, bentonite, opal and gold. After 2 miles you'll see a tunnel on the left. Take a look, but don't venture inside. Keep right at 3.6 miles. At 4 miles you'll reach a saddle. Walk up the knoll to the left, and take in a sweeping view of the El Paso Mountains, Black Hills and Last Chance Canyon. Your route will veer left from the knoll, past Gerbracht Camp and down into the canyon. About 2.8 miles from the saddle you'll see a sign for the tunnel at a fork. Go left, and in another 0.7 miles you'll be at Tonie Seger's cabin. The tunnel is about 200 yards farther. Let Mrs. Seger show you the cabin of the late prospector William H. "Burro" Schmidt, who spent 34 years on the project. There's no fee, but donations are welcome.

REST STOPS: Camping at Red Rock Canyon State Park, where you can ask about 4x4 routes. Inyokern, to the north, has a park on Sunset Avenue. Visit the old mining town of Randsburg, where the historic General Store & Boarding House has a soda fountain. Tour Last Chance Canyon.

GETTING HOME: Highway 14 or U.S. 395.

MAPS: BLM's Red Mountain Desert Access Guide or Hileman's Gem, Mineral & 4-Wheel Drive Map of Last Chance Canyon, Mesquite Canyon and Iron Canyon.

INFORMATION: Burro Schmidt's Tunnel, KMX 7017, P.O. Box H, Randsburg, CA 93554; BLM, Ridgecrest, 619-384-5400.

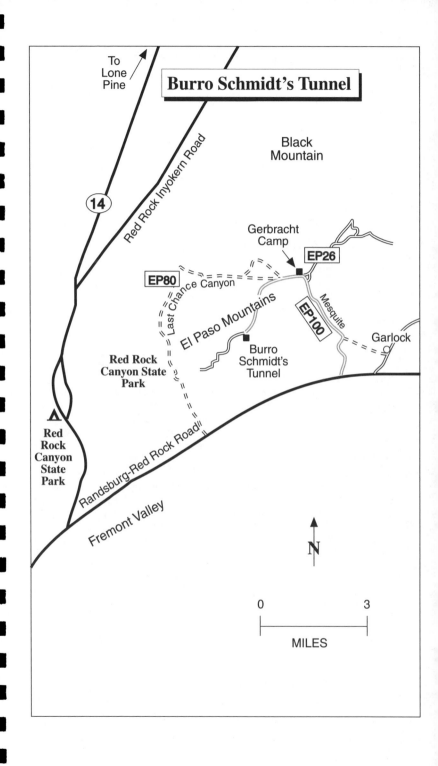

Burro Schmidt's Tunnel

To Lone Pine

Black Mountain

Red Rock Inyokern Road

14

Gerbracht Camp

EP26

EP80

Last Chance Canyon

El Paso Mountains

EP100

Mesquite

Garlock

Red Rock Canyon State Park

Burro Schmidt's Tunnel

Red Rock Canyon State Park

Randsburg-Red Rock Road

Fremont Valley

N

0   3
MILES

Red Rock Canyon S.P.

LOCATION: Off state Highway 14 about 25 miles north of Mojave.

HIGHLIGHTS: The namesake canyon of this unusual state park consists of gorgeous, intricately eroded cliffs and colorful badlands that have been popular with movie makers. The shadeless campground is neat. Great views. Natural preserves.

DIFFICULTY: This loop is easy, but there is one moderate sandy wash toward the end that's about a quarter-mile long.

TIME & DISTANCE: An hour; 7.3 miles.

GETTING THERE: Take Abbott Drive 0.8 mile north of the turnoff to the campground and visitor center. Turn left onto Dove Spring Road. Set your odometer at 0.

THE DRIVE: During the 1870s, the colorful formations you'll see in this park were a landmark for 20-mule team freight wagons, which stopped here for water. But archaeological evidence shows that native people passed through this juncture of the El Paso Range and the southernmost tip of the Sierra Nevada Mountains 15,000 to 20,000 years ago. This park also is a biological transition area between the Mojave Desert and the Sierra Nevada Mountains where species from both areas live. At 0.2 miles from the start, you'll come to a fork. Keep left, out of the sand. Soon you'll enter the Dove Spring Off-Highway Vehicle area. At 0.95 mile, just after you enter the OHV area, turn left toward the powerlines, and keep left. You will drive through an undulating landscape as you more or less follow the power poles. At 3.1 miles you'll come to an intersection of OHV trails. Go directly under the power lines and through a gate. Close the gate behind you. Notice the excellent vista of the desert below. You'll descend to a sandy wash. It's somewhat downhill, so you shouldn't have any trouble. Keep the momentum up. Toward the end of it the road will veer left up an embankment. At 6.6 miles you'll reach a left fork. It goes to Red Rooster Spring, a popular area for viewing spring wildflowers. You'll see Highway 14. Keep left, and you'll soon reach it.

REST STOPS: The park itself, including the 50-site campground at the base of spectacular White House Cliffs.

GETTING HOME: Highway 14.

MAP: BLM's Jawbone/Dove Springs Desert Access Guide.

INFORMATION: Stop at the visitor center for information about various dirt roads in the park. For other information about the park call 805-942-0662.

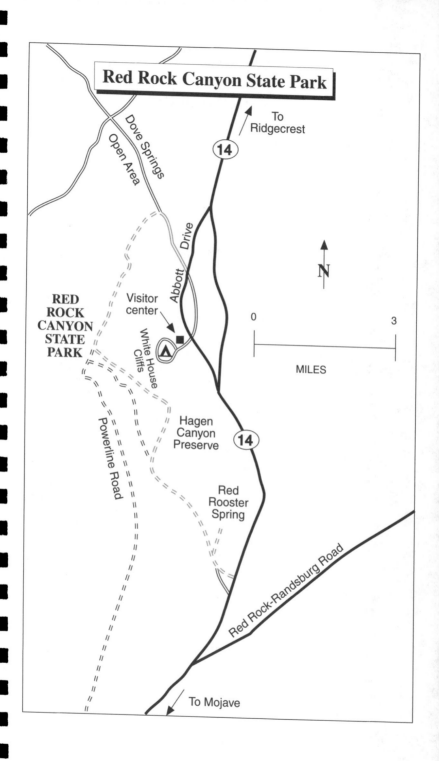

Red Rock Canyon State Park

Alphie Canyon

LOCATION: West of state Highway 14 and Red Rock Canyon State Park.

HIGHLIGHTS: A pretty canyon that is easily accessible and great for breaking up the highway miles.

DIFFICULTY: Easy.

TIME & DISTANCE: 1.5 hours or less; 18.4 miles round–trip from Highway 14.

GETTING THERE: From Highway 14 a little more than a mile south of the Red Rock-Randsburg Road, take the Jawbone Canyon/Kelso Valley turnoff.

THE DRIVE: You'll take the Kelso Valley Road. At 4.1 miles up Jawbone Canyon, after you pass two large pipelines of the Los Angeles Aqueduct, the pavement ends. You can see a large blue/gray hillside ahead, Blue Point, which derives its color from copper. It's near the entrance to Alphie Canyon, which you'll reach at 4.7 miles. Turn right onto road SC176, indicated by a signpost. The canyon entrance is in the Jawbone Canyon Off-Highway Vehicle area, and you may have some company. After 0.75 mile, as you cross a wash, a branch will go left. It's SC 251, but continue straight on SC176. You'll go over a series of "whoops," or bumps as you pass rust–colored rock. Soon you'll see another fork. SC176 continues straight, into the rocks. You'll pass some massive red rocks. If it's shady there, have lunch. You'll also see places here and there where the rock is smoothed by occasional waterfalls. In case you haven't noticed, this canyon seems overpopulated by jackrabbits. Counting them as they dart in front of you can be a great pastime for the kids. Also watch for coyotes. The driveable road ends about 4.5 miles from the Kelso Valley Road, unless you're piloting a genuine off-road vehicle.

REST STOPS: Anywhere along the way. Red Rock Canyon State Park is a few miles north on Highway 14.

GETTING HOME: Return to Highway 14.

MAP: BLM's Jawbone/Dove Springs Desert Access Guide.

INFORMATION: BLM, Ridgecrest, 619-384-5400.

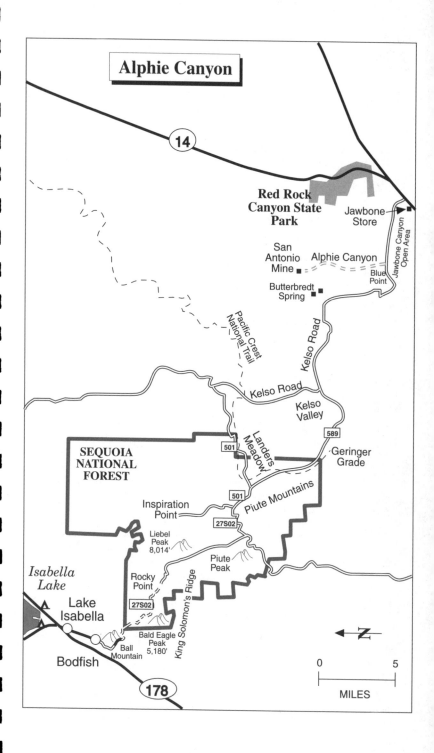

Alphie Canyon

14

Red Rock
Canyon State
Park

Jawbone
Store

San
Antonio
Mine   Alphie Canyon

Blue
Point

Jawbone Canyon Open Area

Butterbredt
Spring

Pacific Crest National Trail

Kelso Road

Kelso Road

Kelso
Valley

589

Landers
Meadow

501

Geringer
Grade

SEQUOIA
NATIONAL
FOREST

501

Inspiration
Point

Piute Mountains

27S02

Liebel
Peak
8,014'

Piute
Peak

Rocky
Point

27S02

Isabella
Lake

Lake
Isabella

King Solomon's Ridge

Bald Eagle
Peak
5,180'

Bodfish

Ball
Mountain

178

N

0   5

MILES

Jawbone to Lake Isabella

LOCATION: From state Highway 14 south of Red Rock Canyon State Park northwest to Lake Isabella.

HIGHLIGHTS: Beautiful, fascinating transition from the Mojave Desert to the pine forests of the southern Sierras. Side trip up Alphie Canyon. Stunning descent to Lake Isabella.

DIFFICULTY: Easy.

TIME & DISTANCE: 6 hours; 65 miles.

GETTING THERE: From Highway 14 about a mile south of Red Rock-Randsburg Road, take the Jawbone Canyon/Kelso Valley turnoff.

THE DRIVE: You'll start out on the Kelso Road at about 2,500 feet elevation, and ultimately climb higher than 8,000 feet. At 4.1 miles up Jawbone Canyon, after you pass two large pipelines of the Los Angeles Aqueduct, the pavement ends. You'll see a blue-gray hill ahead, Blue Point. It's near the entrance to Alphie Canyon, which you'll reach at 4.7 miles. It's a scenic, 9-mile round-trip drive. Eventually you'll make a steep but easy climb into desert mountains. At 7.1 miles from Alphie Canyon you'll come to road SC123 to Butterbredt Canyon and spring. The latter is private land maintained as a wildlife sanctuary by Onyx Ranch and the National Audubon Society. Continuing, aridity begins to give way to vegetation. Soon you're descending into pastoral Kelso Valley. About 6.2 miles from the Butterbredt turnoff, go through the intersection even though the sign says Isabella is right. Cross Kelso Valley Road, then a long, grassy meadow and climb into the Piute Mountains, passing through an idyllic landscape. Go up Geringer Grade, crossing into Sequoia National Forest. You'll eventually round a bend, and suddenly see a vista of the southern Sierra. About 1.6 miles farther you'll pass road 29S02 on the left. Continue straight toward Piute Mountain Road, about 3.1 miles farther. Go left (west) when you reach it. It's road 501 on Sequoia National Forest's map. Driving through pine forest, you'll pass the left (south) turn to Piute Peak. Continue on road 27S02 toward Bodfish.

REST STOPS: Boating, camping, etc., at the lake.

GETTING HOME: Highway 178 east to Highway 14, west to Bakersfield.

MAPS: BLM's Jawbone/Dove Springs Desert Access Guide. Sequoia National Forest.

INFORMATION: BLM, Ridgecrest, 619-384-5400. Sequoia N.F., Greenhorn Ranger District, 805-871-2223.

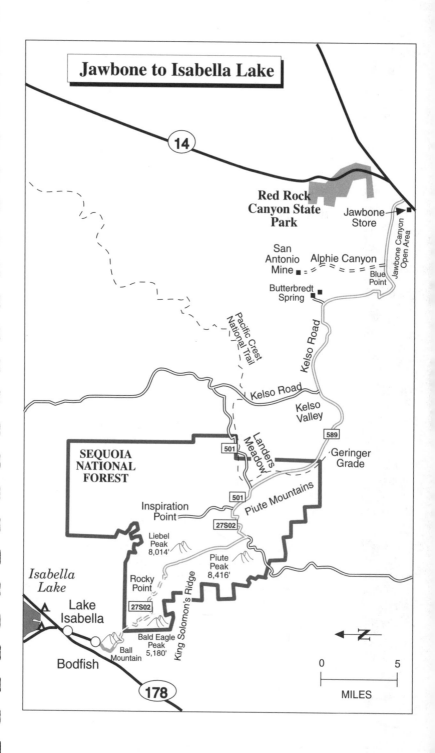

Jawbone to Isabella Lake

14

Red Rock Canyon State Park

Jawbone Store

San Antonio Mine

Alphie Canyon

Blue Point

Butterbredt Spring

Jawbone Canyon Open Area

Pacific Crest National Trail

Kelso Road

Kelso Road

Kelso Valley

589

Landers Meadow

501

Geringer Grade

SEQUOIA NATIONAL FOREST

501

Inspiration Point

Piute Mountains

27S02

Liebel Peak 8,014'

Piute Peak 8,416'

Rocky Point

27S02

King Solomon's Ridge

Isabella Lake

Lake Isabella

Bald Eagle Peak 5,180'

Ball Mountain

Bodfish

178

N

0   5

MILES

Inscription Canyon Loop

LOCATION: 30 miles northwest of Barstow.

HIGHLIGHTS: Fine petroglyphs. Black Canyon. Adjacent Black Mountain Wilderness. Rainbow Basin is spectacular.

DIFFICULTY: Easy, but there is sand in Black Canyon. Once out of Black Canyon navigation will be tricky. Bring a compass and follow the map closely.

TIME & DISTANCE: 6 to 7 hours; 70 miles.

GETTING THERE: From Barstow, take Irwin Road north about 7 miles; turn left at the sign for Rainbow Basin; drive another 3 miles. After taking the drive through the basin, return to Irwin Road for the trek to Inscription, Black canyons.

THE DRIVE: The 4-mile drive through the colorful formations of Rainbow Basin is tops. Return to Irwin Road; turn left (northeast). Drive a little more than a mile; turn left onto Copper City Road. Go 16.4 miles across rolling desert marked by numerous volcanic domes to a 4-way intersection. Go left (west) to Superior Valley on road EF373, Copper City Road. You'll pass some side routes, but stay on EF373 for 9.3 miles. The dirt road gradually narrows as you approach Inscription Canyon. You'll see a barrier at the mouth of the small canyon, which is about 200 yards long. You'll see many petroglyphs, and much vandalism. Drive the two-track north around the canyon, watching for more petroglyphs. This road will soon curve south. About 2.1 miles from the canyon you'll reach a Y; keep right. You'll soon enter scenic Black Canyon. The east (left) side of the road is the wilderness boundary. The road, still EF373, is now called Black Canyon Road. You'll begin a 2-mile sandy stretch, but you're descending, which should make it easy. When you leave the canyon you'll reach a junction. Road EF373 continues south across a flat, passing to the left of a large tree and reaching road EF401 at a fence line. Go left (east), toward the green farmland in the distance. Follow the fence line, which will be on your right. As you pass the farm the road will angle right (southeast). You'll see utility poles along the road. Follow the road southeast. About 10 miles from the farm, go left at a Y. Rainbow Basin and Irwin Road are ahead.

REST STOPS: Owl Canyon C.G. at Rainbow Basin.

GETTING HOME: Irwin Road to Barstow.

MAPS: BLM's Red Mt., Irwin, Stoddard Valley maps.

INFORMATION: California Desert Information Center, 619-255-8760; BLM, Barstow, 619-255-8700.

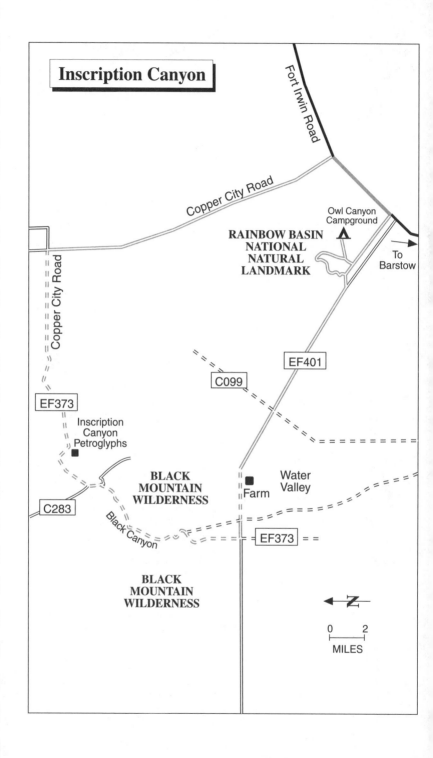

Inscription Canyon

Fort Irwin Road

Copper City Road

Copper City Road

Owl Canyon Campground

RAINBOW BASIN NATIONAL NATURAL LANDMARK

To Barstow

EF401

C099

EF373

Inscription Canyon Petroglyphs

BLACK MOUNTAIN WILDERNESS

Water Valley

Farm

C283

Black Canyon

EF373

BLACK MOUNTAIN WILDERNESS

N

0   2
MILES

Cedar Canyon Road

LOCATION: Mojave National Preserve, between Interstates 15 & 40.

HIGHLIGHTS: This road goes through a beautiful high-desert area that is the geographic center of the Mojave Desert.

DIFFICULTY: Easy on graded dirt and gravel.

TIME & DISTANCE: About 1.5 hours; 25 miles.

GETTING THERE: From I-15 about 25.8 miles northeast of Baker, take the Cima Road exit. Go right. Drive 22.1 miles, through Cima; turn left (east) on Cedar Canyon Road.

THE DRIVE: On Cima Road, you'll climb gradually to a saddle, at about 5,100 feet elevation. You'll see a hiking trail westward to Teutonia Peak (2 miles). Looking out that way, you're seeing Cima Dome. It was formed when a core of molten rock cooled and the overlying rock was stripped away by erosion. Then the exposed granite core was eroded. The Cedar Canyon Road will take you through the Mid Hills along the historic Mojave Road. About 2.5 miles from where you turned onto Cedar Canyon Road the pavement quits and you're on a good graded dirt and gravel road. Before you enter the canyon, stop and view the panorama of the East Mojave region. You'll descend into the canyon as the road narrows. About 6 miles from the start you'll reach the south turn to Black Canyon Road. It will take you to Wild Horse Canyon, and to campgrounds at Mid Hills (5 miles away) and Hole-In-The-Wall (10 miles away). Both campgrounds have water. You'll pass through Round Valley, at about 5,000 feet. To the north is Pinto Mountain. The butte to the south is Table Mountain. As the road descends and crosses Watson Wash, south of the road will be Rock Spring, a watering hole along the Mojave Road (check your map) that also was used by Indians for thousands of years. The Army had a camp near here in the 1800s. You'll come out at the Ivanpah-Lanfair Road.

REST STOPS: Mid Hills, Hole-In-The-Wall campgrounds. Rock Spring, where there are petroglyphs and old Army graffiti. (It's illegal to deface, remove or in any way disturb archaeological and historic artifacts.)

GETTING HOME: From the junction with the Ivanpah-Lanfair Byway, it's 27 miles to I-40. Or take the Ivanpah-Lanfair Byway 33 miles north to I-15.

MAP: BLM's New York Mountains Desert Access Guide.

INFORMATION: Mojave Desert Information Center in Baker, 619-733-4040.

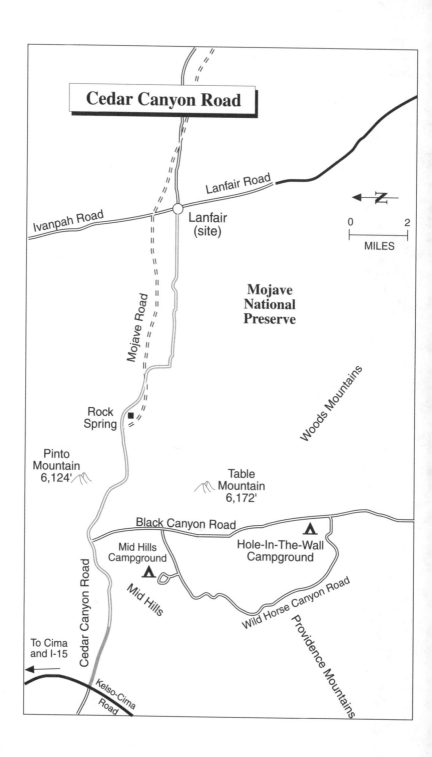

Cedar Canyon Road

Afton Canyon

LOCATION: 37 miles east of Barstow; south of I-15.

HIGHLIGHTS: Multicolored rock canyon along the Mojave River; side canyons to explore on foot.

DIFFICULTY: Easy to moderate. Air your tires down to 16-18 pounds for better traction. The route follows the bed of the Mojave River. If the weather is hot and dry, turning the sand to potentially treacherous powder, choose tracks on firm ground. If the riverbed sand is damp, it might be firmer. Drive on the sandbars. Stay out of the riverbed if it's flooded.

TIME & DISTANCE: 2 to 3 hours; 10 miles round-trip.

GETTING THERE: Take I-15 east 37 miles from Barstow. Take the Afton Road exit; go right on gravel Afton Canyon Road 3.4 miles to a campground. Set your odometer at 0 there.

THE DRIVE: This beautiful, colorful canyon was created about 19,000 years ago when Lake Manix drained. The fluted canyon walls rise about 300 feet above the Mojave River. This canyon is one of only three places where the Mojave River has surface flow below its headwaters during non-flood periods. The presence of water makes this area critical wildlife habitat, and quite lush by desert standards. Early in the drive you might even have a rare desert experience, fording a pool of water. Parallel the riverbed for a mile. You'll cross the riverbed after going under a railroad bridge. (You're likely to see a few freight trains on this drive.) As you enter the canyon, the railroad tracks will be on your left. The well-marked route, part of the historic Mojave Road, winds along the tracks. 0.6 mile from the railroad bridge the route angles right, dipping into the riverbed. Follow the signs for route AF2525. Here and there you might want to leave the riverbed and get close to the tracks, depending on conditions. Some road sections may be washed out, but there will be alternate tracks. At about mile 5 you'll exit the canyon, and soon reach the Basin railroad siding. On the other side of the river is an old limestone mine. You can drive to it if the riverbed sand is fairly firm, but inspect the crossing first. You might just walk instead. Old mine sites often mean nails in your tires, and they can be dangerous as well.

REST STOPS: Campground has water, pit toilets, tables.

GETTING HOME: Back to I-15.

MAPS: BLM's Irwin Desert Access Guide; for canyon hiking, get the USGS Cave Mountain topographic map.

INFORMATION: BLM, Barstow, 619-255-8700; California Desert Information Center, Barstow, 619-255-8760.

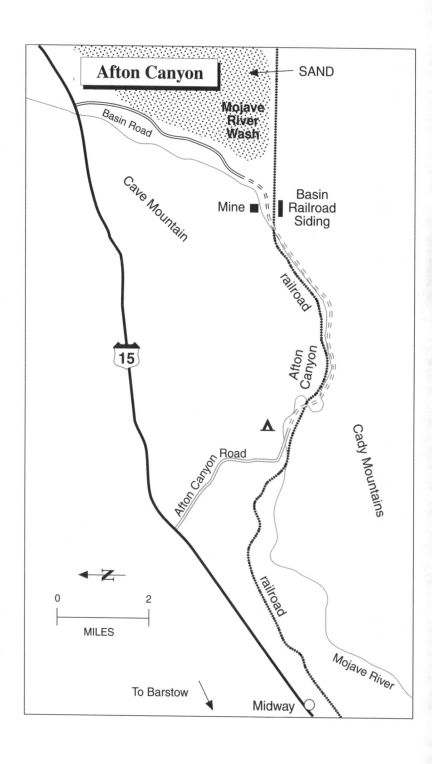

Afton Canyon

SAND

Mojave River Wash

Basin Road

Cave Mountain

Mine

Basin Railroad Siding

railroad

Afton Canyon

Afton Canyon Road

Cady Mountains

N

0   2

MILES

railroad

Mojave River

To Barstow

Midway

Wild Horse Canyon

LOCATION: Mojave National Preserve, between Interstates 15 & 40. Off Black Canyon Road.

HIGHLIGHTS: Getting there, you'll drive through magnificent high desert scenery, go past Wild Horse Mesa and the colorful volcanic formations at Hole-In-The-Wall and Lobo Point.

DIFFICULTY: An easy loop. Flash floods in summer can make the route impassable.

TIME & DISTANCE: 1.5 to 2 hours; 11.7 miles.

GETTING THERE: From I-15, take the Cima Road exit 25.8 miles north of Baker. Go right at the bottom of the exit. Go 17.5 miles southeast to Cima, then veer right. Go 4.6 miles, and turn left (east) onto Cedar Canyon Road. In 6 miles turn right (south) onto Black Canyon Road. In another 2.8 miles turn right (west) toward Mid Hills campground and you're on the route. From I-40, take the exit for Mitchell Caverns and Providence Mountains. Take Essex Road northwest 9.7 miles to Black Canyon Road; turn onto the route after 9.6 miles.

THE DRIVE: This area used to be the East Mojave National Scenic Area. You're at about 5,400 feet. Notice how much cooler it is compared with the low desert you came from? You'll pass through rolling, rocky granite and volcanic hills covered with sagebrush, pinyon and juniper, with spectacular vistas of the desert region, including the jagged peaks of the Providence Mountains, distant ranges and sand dunes.

REST STOPS: Mid Hills and Hole-In-The-Wall campgrounds have water. An unmaintained, 7-mile hiking trail begins at Mid Hills Campground, goes through cactus gardens and rock formations, and ends at the southern segment of this drive. (Its route is not accurately depicted on the Desert Access Guide.) Explore the volcanic formations at Hole-In-The-Wall on a trail from the picnic area. Visit Providence Mountains State Recreation Area, Mitchell Caverns, Kelso Dunes, Cinder Cones National Natural Landmark.

GETTING HOME: I-15 or I-40.

MAP: BLM's New York Mountains Desert Access Guide.

INFORMATION: Mojave Desert Information Center, 619-733-4040.

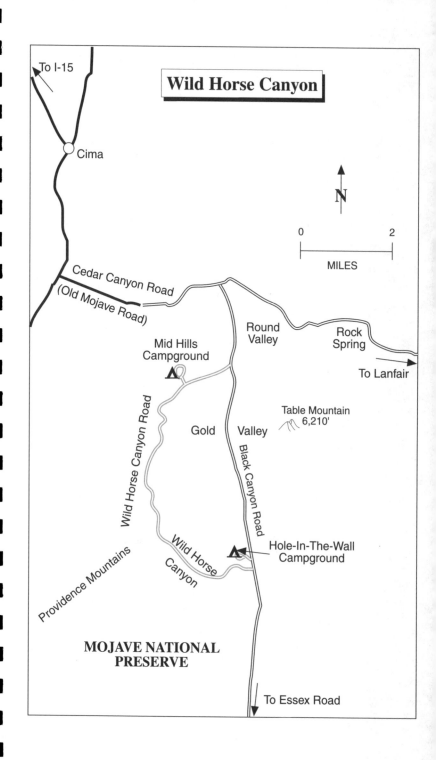

Wild Horse Canyon

To I-15

Cima

N

0   2
MILES

Cedar Canyon Road
(Old Mojave Road)

Round
Valley

Rock
Spring

Mid Hills
Campground

To Lanfair

Table Mountain
6,210'

Gold   Valley

Wild Horse Canyon Road

Black Canyon Road

Wild Horse
Canyon

Hole-In-The-Wall
Campground

Providence Mountains

**MOJAVE NATIONAL
PRESERVE**

To Essex Road

Ivanpah-Lanfair Road

LOCATION: Mojave National Preserve, between Interstates 15 & 40.

HIGHLIGHTS: Fabulous high–desert and desert mountain scenery, including the New York Mountains, Castle Mountains, views of Castle Peaks, Lanfair Valley and Hackberry Mountains. Best in late afternoon light.

DIFFICULTY: Easy. The first and final stretches are paved. The middle 25 miles or so is graded dirt. Watch for floods.

TIME & DISTANCE: 2 hours; 55 miles.

GETTING THERE: From I-15, take the Nipton Road exit. Drive about 3.5 miles east, then turn right (south) on Ivanpah Road. From I-40, take the Goffs Road exit. Drive north 10.4 miles to Goffs. Turn left (northwest) on Lanfair Road.

THE DRIVE: Take this either way, starting from I-15 or I-40. From either direction, you'll climb steadily from less than 3,000 feet elevation to more than 5,000 feet in the beautiful New York Mountains. (New York Mountains Road is the main access for camping, hunting, etc.) You'll cross Fenner and Lanfair valleys, view the rugged ridges and peaks of the Hackberry Mountains, the Vontrigger Hills, Castle Mountains and the volcanic spires of Castle Peaks. About 16.3 miles north of Goffs, you'll come to the intersection with Cedar Canyon Road, described separately. The area around volcanic Castle Peaks has outstanding hiking.

REST STOPS: Backcountry sites in the New York Mountains, particularly Caruthers Canyon, where there's an old mine you can walk to. On I-15, Las Vegas is about 50 miles north, and Baker, Calif., about 40 miles southwest. On I-40, Needles, Calif., is about 40 miles east, and Ludlow about 60 miles west.

GETTING HOME: I-15 or I-40.

MAPS: BLM's New York Mountains and Providence Mountains Desert Access Guides.

INFORMATION: Mojave Desert Information Center, 619-733-4040.

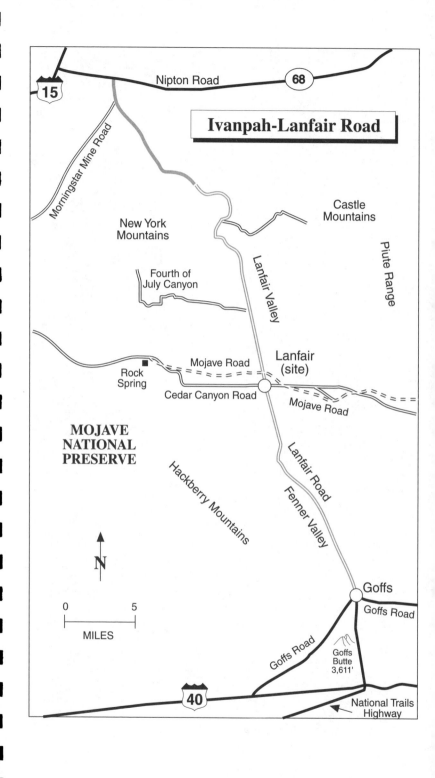

Ivanpah-Lanfair Road

Red Rock Canyon, along the Volcanic Tableland drive.

Petroglyphs at Chidago Canyon, along the Volcanic Tableland drive.

Lunch on Mazourka Peak.

Titus Canyon, Death Valley National Park.

Titus Canyon, Death Valley National Park

The Racetrack, Death Valley National Park.

Searching for The Racetrack's "moving rocks."

Water break at Lost Burro Gap, Death Valley National Park.

Echo Canyon in Death Valley National Park.

Inyo Mine in Echo Canyon, Death Valley National Park.

Not everyone thinks the threatened desert tortoise is worth saving.

Chocolate Mountain Aerial Gunnery Range, along Bradshaw Trail.

Afton Canyon

Borrego Badlands from Font's Point, Anza-Borrego Desert State
Park.

Sandstone Canyon, Anza-Borrego Desert State Park.

Leadfield townsite, Death Valley National Park

Black Canyon Road

LOCATION: Mojave National Preserve.

HIGHLIGHTS: Spectacular high-desert vistas, spring wild-flowers, colorful and bizarre volcanic formations at Hole-In-The-Wall. Outstanding views of Table Mountain, the Providence Mountains, Woods Mountains and Colton Hills.

DIFFICULTY: Easy; quasi-paved road.

TIME & DISTANCE: An hour; 20 miles.

GETTING THERE: From I-15 about 25.8 miles northeast of Baker, take the Cima Road exit. Go right. Drive 22.1 miles, through Cima, and turn east (left) on Cedar Canyon Road. Drive 6 miles, then turn right (south) onto Black Canyon Road. From I-40, take the exit for Mitchell Caverns and Providence Mountains. Follow Essex Road north for 9.7 miles to Black Canyon Road, and turn right (north).

THE DRIVE: I'll describe this going from north to south. You'll start at Cedar Canyon, at about 5,000 feet elevation in the Mid Hills, and immediately cross Cedar Wash. You'll gradually climb about 300 feet through pinyon pine, juniper and sagebrush, and in less than a mile emerge onto a flat. Soon you'll reach the right turn to Wild Horse Canyon, a gorgeous drive described separately. Look off into the hills to the left, and you'll notice that some lucky folks have homes in this magnificent country. Now you're getting great views of Table Mountain, distant ranges and valleys as you pass through a dry canyon. A vast panorama opens up before you as you make a long descent to about 2,500 feet. Speed can creep up on you on these gradual descents, so be careful. Watch out for cattle on the road, too. Soon you'll see the glint of the real world as, far off in the distance, you see traffic moving along I-40 like ants marching through a primeval desert landscape. At Essex Road, Mitchell Caverns is to the right; I-40 and reality are to the left.

REST STOPS: Hole-In-The-Wall campground; Mitchell Caverns and Providence Mountains State Recreation Area.

GETTING HOME: I-15 or I-40.

MAPS: BLM's New York Mountains and Providence Mountains Desert Access Guides.

INFORMATION: Mojave Desert Information Center, 619-733-4040.

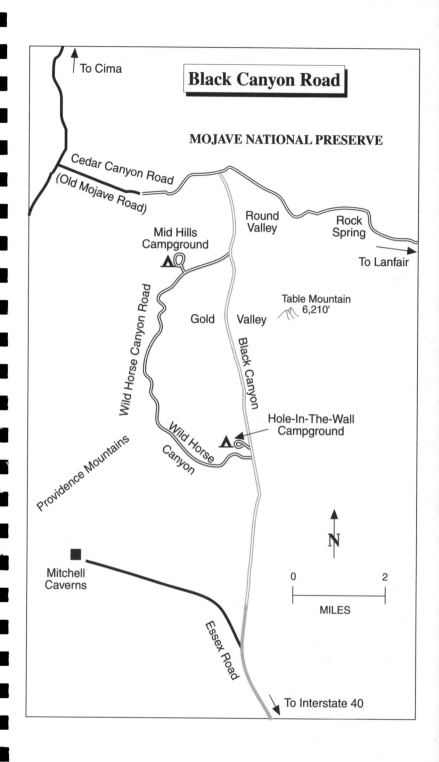

Black Canyon Road

MOJAVE NATIONAL PRESERVE

To Cima

Cedar Canyon Road
(Old Mojave Road)

Round Valley

Rock Spring

To Lanfair

Mid Hills Campground

Table Mountain
6,210'

Gold Valley

Wild Horse Canyon Road

Black Canyon

Hole-In-The-Wall Campground

Wild Horse Canyon

Providence Mountains

Mitchell Caverns

N

0   2

MILES

Essex Road

To Interstate 40

Mojave Road

LOCATION: It begins on the west bank of the Colorado River in Nevada at the Fort Mojave Indian Reservation north of Needles, Calif. It goes west through Mojave National Preserve. It ends east of Barstow on I-15, at Manix near the site of the 19th century Army outpost, Camp Cady.

HIGHLIGHTS: Magnificent scenery in Mojave National Preserve and Afton Canyon; historic ruins, petroglyphs and geologic sites.

DIFFICULTY: Easy to moderate. However, there are stretches that can be treacherously sandy or muddy, including Soda Lake, the Mojave River flood plain and Afton Canyon. You may have to detour around them.

TIME & DISTANCE: 2 to 3 days if you drive the entire 138-mile route, which for safety should be done with more than one vehicle. You can also drive segments of it.

GETTING THERE: Segments of the road are accessible at a number of points in the eastern Mojave Desert. (Refer to your maps.) From the bridge over I-40 at Needles, take River Road north toward Laughlin, Nev. It will become Pew Road after 5.6 miles. Drive another 10.25 miles. Then you can go left (west) onto the Mojave Road. But the real starting point is at the river, 3 miles to the right.

THE DRIVE: This historic road began as an Indian trail with reliable sources of water. From explorers like Jedediah Smith to prospectors and Army troops, all sorts of people who moved West in the 1800s used it. In the 1980s it was restored for public use by author and historian Dennis Casebier and the Friends of the Mojave Road. It climbs from under 500 feet elevation at the start to over 5,000 feet in Mojave National Preserve. It passes through a rich variety of desert vegetation and historic sites like the rock remains of an 1860s Army outpost, Fort Piute, and ancient petroglyphs.

REST STOPS: There's a telephone at Lanfair. The campgrounds at Mid Hills and Hole-In-The-Wall have water.

MAPS: BLM's Needles, New York Mountains, Irwin & Johnson Valley Desert Access Guides.

INFORMATION: Mojave Desert Information Center, 619-733-4040; Friends of the Mojave Road, 619-733-4482. Don't go without a copy of the Mojave Road Guide, by Dennis G. Casebier and the Friends. It's available locally, or you can order it from the Friends at the address listed in this book.

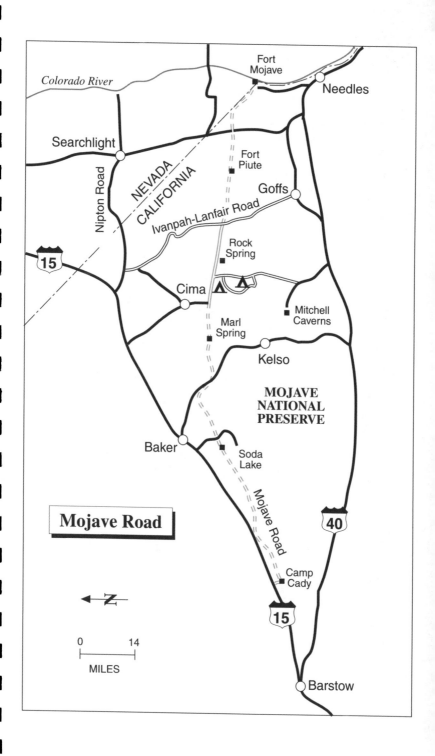

Mojave Road

N

0   14
MILES

Stoddard Well Road

LOCATION: Between Victorville and Barstow.

HIGHLIGHTS: Vistas of a vast desert landscape of volcanic mountains and broad valleys. A great alternative to the freeways.

DIFFICULTY: The graded dirt road couldn't be easier. Take in either direction.

TIME & DISTANCE: 1 hour; 26.5 miles.

GETTING THERE: From I-15 north of Victorville, take the Stoddard Well Road exit. From Barstow, take Barstow Road (state Highway 247) south about six miles, then turn right (west) onto Stoddard Well Road.

THE DRIVE: If you're looking for a relaxing cruise through remote, rolling desert, this is it. Going from Victorville, the road parallels I-15 for about 3.5 miles, then veers northeast. The pavement ends after about 7.6 miles, and 2.5 miles later you're in the desert hills and mountains, and then Stoddard Valley. The road passes through the 33,500-acre Stoddard Valley Off–Highway Vehicle Area, where cross-country driving is allowed. You'll see the scars. When you reach Barstow Road, go left (north).

REST STOPS: The California Desert Information Center on Barstow Road in Barstow, or the nice park across the street from it. In Victorville, the Mojave Narrows County Regional Park.

GETTING HOME: I-15 at Victorville; I-15 or I-40 at Barstow.

MAP: BLM's Stoddard Valley Desert Access Guide.

INFORMATION: California Desert Information Center in Barstow, 619-255-8760.

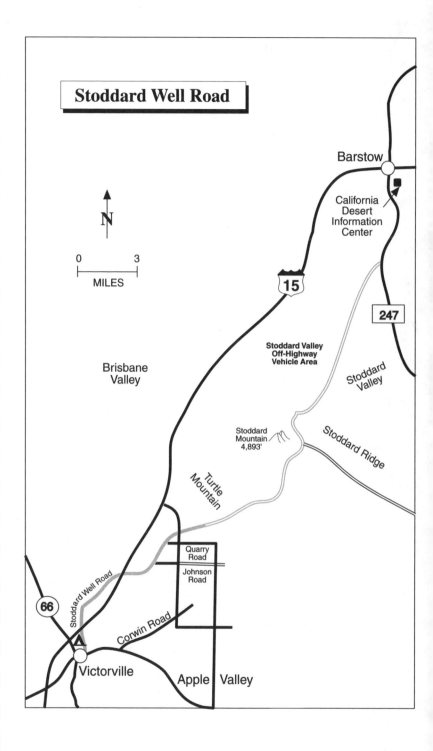

Stoddard Well Road

N

0 3
MILES

Barstow

California Desert Information Center

15

247

Brisbane Valley

Stoddard Valley Off-Highway Vehicle Area

Stoddard Valley

Stoddard Mountain 4,893'

Stoddard Ridge

Turtle Mountain

Stoddard Well Road

Quarry Road

Johnson Road

66

Corwin Road

Victorville

Apple Valley

Rodman Mountains Loop

LOCATION: South of I-40, east of Barstow.

HIGHLIGHTS: Rock art at Surprise Tank; Box Canyon.

DIFFICULTY: Easy to moderate; some sandy stretches.

TIME & DISTANCE: 4 hours; 40 miles.

GETTING THERE: Take I-40 east from Barstow for 5.6 miles. Take the Daggett exit; go right. Go left on Pendleton Road. When the asphalt ends Pendleton becomes Camp Rock Road. Set your odometer at 0 here. Or take Camp Rock Road east of Victorville, described separately.

THE DRIVE: The graded dirt road climbs into rolling hills. (Watch out for large trucks.) You'll go through a small canyon and then into a long valley between the Newberry and Ord Mountains. After 17.1 miles Camp Rock Road veers southwest. Go straight, on road OJ228. After another mile go left. Just as you approach the mining operation at a cinder cone, take a small dirt road on the right, OJ233. Just beyond a ravine the road will fork to the right. To the left, toward the newly designated Rodman Mountains Wilderness, are two fenced areas protecting prehistoric Indian geoglyphs, or rocks aligned into shapes on the ground. The first is what appears to be a ram's horns. The site also includes the distinct track of an ancient footpath that looks like a motorcycle track. The second fenced area protects the shape of a large boomerang. A short distance to the southeast is a fissure, the Surprise Tank petroglyph site. The "tank" collects water, when there is any. Look on the fissure's walls for the petroglyphs. It's best if you continue down the main route 0.8 mile farther, and go left on a somewhat rough two-track to a parking area at the south end of the tank, and then tour the sites. About 2.7 miles farther, at an intersection, go left under the powerlines, then left again after a short distance on road OJ295. You'll enter Box Canyon. On either side is wilderness. The canyon ends as you pass through a gap and, still in the wilderness, emerge onto a slope overlooking I-40. Drive down the wash to the dirt gas pipeline road. Go left (west). Then go right (north) after 1.6 miles, at the pipeline substation. Go to the paved road, then left to I-40.

REST STOPS: Surprise Tank and Box Canyon.

GETTING HOME: I-40 or I-15 at Barstow; or follow Camp Rock Road southwest to Hwy. 247 and Lucerne Valley.

MAP: BLM's Johnson Valley Desert Access Guide.

INFORMATION: California Desert Information Center in Barstow, 619-255-8760; BLM, Barstow, 619-255-8700.

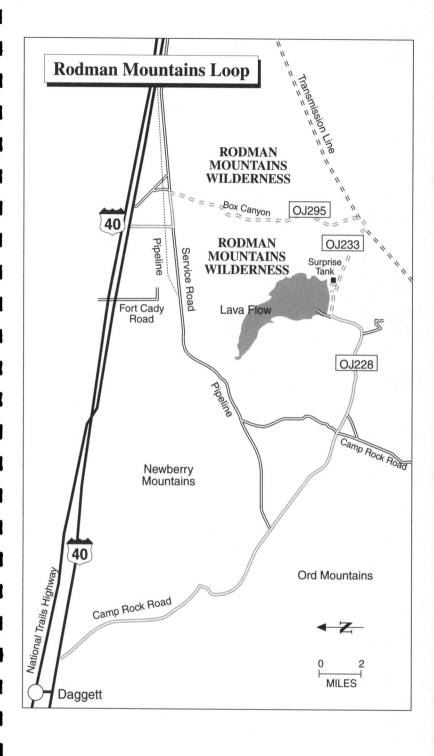

Rodman Mountains Loop

RODMAN MOUNTAINS WILDERNESS

Transmission Line

Box Canyon OJ295

RODMAN MOUNTAINS WILDERNESS

OJ233

Surprise Tank

Lava Flow

OJ228

Pipeline

Service Road

Fort Cady Road

Pipeline

Newberry Mountains

Camp Rock Road

Ord Mountains

N

0 2
MILES

National Trails Highway

Camp Rock Road

Daggett

Camp Rock Road

LOCATION: South of Interstate 40, north of state Highway 247; east of Barstow and Victorville.

HIGHLIGHTS: Fine scenery of mountains and broad valleys; petroglyphs at Surprise Tank. Side trip to Cougar Buttes. Great alternative to the freeways. Take in either direction.

DIFFICULTY: Easy.

TIME & DISTANCE: 2.5 to 3 hours; 47 miles.

GETTING THERE: From Victorville, take state Hwy. 18 to Lucerne Valley; continue east on Hwy. 247. Almost 6.5 miles farther, where the highway bends southeast, Camp Rock Road goes north.

THE DRIVE: The first 10.2 miles are paved as the road heads straight into volcanic hills. You'll notice the jagged cluster of rocks to the east, Cougar Buttes. They're neat, so turn right at Cambria Road to visit them. Camp Rock eventually will branch off to the right (northeast), and Harrod Road will continue north. Unpaved Camp Rock Road is wide and very good as you pass between the Ord Mountains on your left and the Fry Mountains on your right. Soon you'll pass through the Johnson Valley Off-Highway Vehicle Area, where off-road enthusiasts can truly get off-road. About 22 miles from the start of this drive, you can turn right toward a cinder mine. (Watch out for large trucks.) About 6 miles farther, before the cinder mine, turn right onto a single-lane road, OJ233. Shortly after you pass through a volcanic ravine, you'll see a left fork from the main road. It'll take you to two fenced areas that protect ancient geoglyphs, or rocks arranged on the ground into art forms, and to a serene volcanic fissure called Surprise Tank, where the walls bear petroglyphs. (See the Rodman Mountains Loop drive, described separately.) Returning to Camp Rock Road, you'll have a beautiful drive through high desert valleys for about 18 miles to I-40 at Daggett.

REST STOPS: Surprise Tank. There's a lovely park at Lucerne Valley. Barstow has a park across Barstow Road from the California Desert Information Center.

GETTING HOME: I-40. Barstow is 5.6 miles west.

MAPS: BLM's Johnson Valley, Yucca Valley Desert Access Guides.

INFORMATION: California Desert Information Center in Barstow, 619-255-8760.

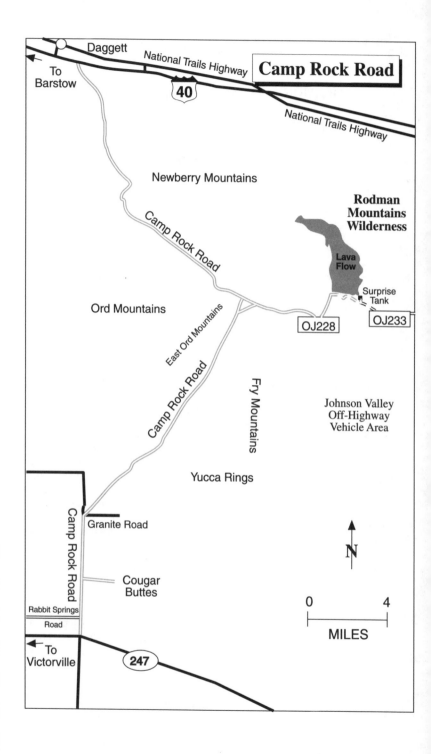

Camp Rock Road

Daggett
To Barstow
National Trails Highway
40
National Trails Highway

Newberry Mountains

Camp Rock Road

Rodman Mountains Wilderness

Lava Flow

Surprise Tank

Ord Mountains

East Ord Mountains

OJ228

OJ233

Camp Rock Road

Fry Mountains

Johnson Valley Off-Highway Vehicle Area

Yucca Rings

N

Camp Rock Road

Granite Road

Cougar Buttes

0   4

MILES

Rabbit Springs Road

To Victorville

247

Big Bear Road

LOCATION: Between Yucca Valley & Baldwin Lake.

HIGHLIGHTS: Varied scenery as you climb from about 4,140 feet elevation in the Mojave high desert to as high as 7,300 feet into the forested San Bernardino Mountains. Perhaps the largest Joshua trees you'll ever see. Beautiful Burns Canyon. Old mining area.

DIFFICULTY: Easy; one short moderate stretch.

TIME & DISTANCE: 4 hours; about 27 miles.

GETTING THERE: From Palm Springs, take state Highway 62 northeast to Yucca Valley. Take Pioneertown Road northwest to Pipes Canyon Road, but go straight onto Rimrock Road instead. It will make a sharp bend to the left, and in 0.8 mile the pavement ends. Set your odometer at 0 here. From the north, take Highway 247 southeast beyond Flamingo Heights. Go west on Pipes Canyon Road for 6.6 miles, then right onto Rimrock.

THE DRIVE: You'll pass through a residential area and dense Joshua tree forest (the real big ones come later), then head up Burns Canyon, crossing a wash several times. About 4.9 miles from the end of the pavement you'll come to a fork. Go right, following the orange arrows on the Joshua trees. At about 6 miles you'll reach an intersection. Go left, toward Big Bear City. After another 0.4 miles the road to Mound Springs and the large Joshuas branches right. You'll see the Farrington Observatory off to the right, then you'll cross a cattle guard; you're on road 3N06. Veer left, and you'll enter a valley with many exceptionally large Joshuas. Retrace your route to continue on Big Bear Road. You'll enter San Bernardino National Forest, climbing steeply through churned up mountains of fractured granite. About 4.4 miles from where you rejoined Big Bear Road, you'll reach an intersection at the old Rose Mine. You can go straight on road 3N03 for 8.5 miles to Highway 18, but the more scenic route is to go left on 2N01 for 6 miles, crossing pretty Broom Flat to come out on Highway 38.

REST STOPS: There are places along the way, particularly at the Rose Mine area. Big Bear Lake has all services. High Desert Nature Museum in Yucca Valley.

GETTING HOME: Highways 18 or 38.

MAPS: BLM's Yucca Valley Desert Access Guide; San Bernardino National Forest.

INFORMATION: San Bernardino National Forest, Big Bear District, 714-866-3437.

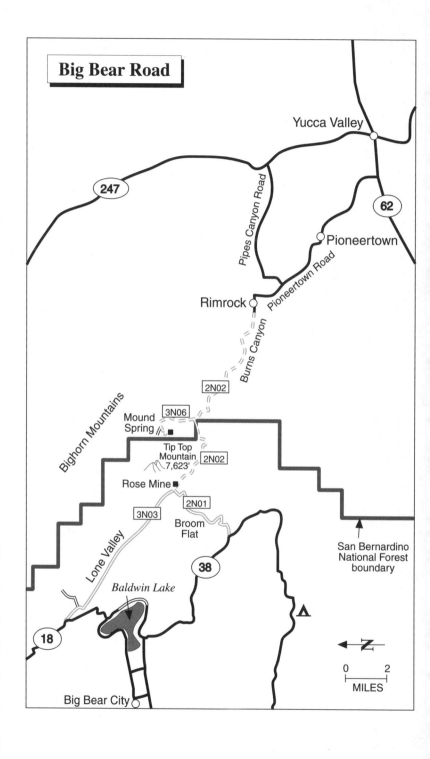

Big Bear Road

Covington Flats

LOCATION: Joshua Tree National Park.

HIGHLIGHTS: A great vista point at the end.

DIFFICULTY: Easy.

TIME & DISTANCE: 1.5 hours; 23 miles.

GETTING THERE: From Yucca Valley, drive 2.7 miles east on Highway 62 from the junction of Highway 247. Turn south on La Contenta Road, going about a mile and straight across Yucca Trail. Set your odometer at 0.

THE DRIVE: Dirt La Contenta passes through a residential area, then veers left after about 1.8 miles. You'll pass Joshua trees and cacti. By 5 miles you're in a burned area, and there are few things that look stranger than the black and white remains of a burned Joshua tree. (The Park Service burned the area deliberately to create a fire break to keep wildfires from reaching inhabited areas.) At 7.7 miles turn right to reach a vista point that provides an excellent view westward of desert valleys and the Little San Bernardino Mountains, from 5,516 feet elevation. The branch southeast from the viewpoint goes to a wilderness trailhead. Beyond the viewpoint turnoff the main road ends in about half a mile.

REST STOPS: The viewpoint.

GETTING HOME: Retrace your route.

MAPS: BLM's Yucca Valley Desert Access Guide and the park brochure.

INFORMATION: Joshua Tree National Park, 619-367-7511.

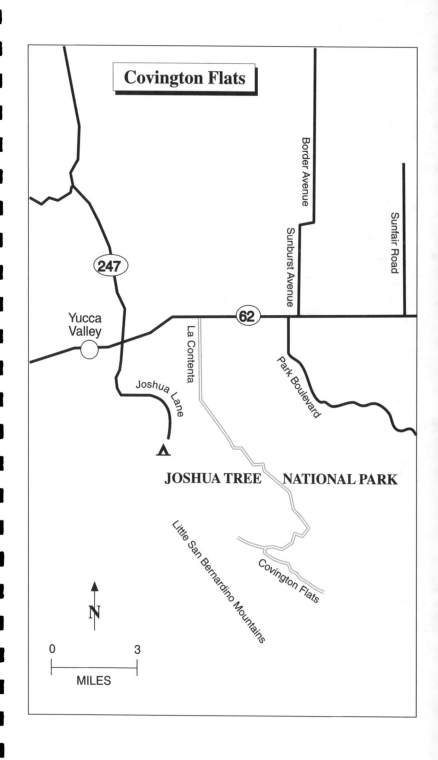

Covington Flats

Border Avenue

Sunfair Road

Sunburst Avenue

247

Yucca Valley

La Contenta

62

Joshua Lane

Park Boulevard

JOSHUA TREE NATIONAL PARK

Little San Bernardino Mountains

Covington Flats

N

0   3
MILES

Geology Tour

LOCATION: Joshua Tree National Park.

HIGHLIGHTS: In a single drive, a chance to see and learn about the park's complex geology and human history.

DIFFICULTY: Easy; conditions can change, though.

TIME & DISTANCE: 2 hours; 17.1 miles.

GETTING THERE: From the towns of Joshua Tree or Twentynine Palms, on state Highway 62, drive south toward Jumbo Rocks. If you're coming from the south, take I-10 east to the Cottonwood Spring Road exit. Go north then northwest. The drive starts west of Jumbo Rocks. Set your odometer at 0 at the start of the route.

THE DRIVE: Pick up the interpretive brochure at the start, or at the visitor centers. It describes 16 points along the way. For the first 4 miles you'll pass among massive boulders and rolling hills in Queen Valley. At 5.4 miles you'll reach the pullout for Squaw Tank, where there are toilets. From about 1000 A.D. to the turn of the century, Native Americans inhabited the area, and Squaw Tank was a favorite spot. In the desert the term "tank" refers to natural basins that collect water after rains. Walk in. You'll see the concrete dams that ranchers built to hold water for their cattle in the early 1900s. There are petroglyphs, and bowl-like mortars Indians made in the rock to grind seeds and other foods into meal. You'll also see old mine remains. When you come to a fork in the road keep left, making your way along the one-way loop across a dry lakebed. (If it's wet, turn back.) At 7.85 miles you'll pass the left turn to Berdoo Canyon Road (1.5 hours; 15.2 miles; moderate). It passes through a rugged canyon and ends at Dillon Road, north of I-10, after descending 3,400 ft. from the high Mojave Desert to the low-lying Colorado Desert. Keep right here to continue the Geology Tour. The loop reconnects with the main tour road.

REST STOPS: There are some very nice campgrounds in the park. Jumbo Rocks is great.

GETTING HOME: North to Highway 62 or south to I-10.

MAPS: BLM's Palm Springs Desert Access Guide; park's map. Be sure to get the brochure "Geology and Man," at the start of the drive, or at the Oasis or Cottonwood visitor centers.

INFORMATION: Joshua Tree National Park, 619-367-7511. Inquire about other routes in the park, such as the Covington Flats, Old Dale Road and Pinkham Canyon drives described in this book.

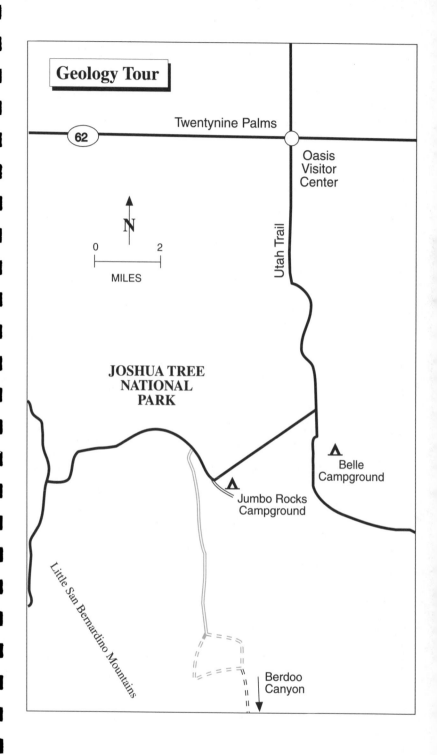

Geology Tour

62 Twentynine Palms

Oasis Visitor Center

Utah Trail

N

0   2

MILES

JOSHUA TREE NATIONAL PARK

Belle Campground

Jumbo Rocks Campground

Little San Bernardino Mountains

Berdoo Canyon

Old Dale Mining District

LOCATION: Joshua Tree National Park and adjacent areas.

HIGHLIGHTS: Remains of the Dale gold mining district; vistas of Pinto Basin.

DIFFICULTY: Easy, with a rough spot or two.

TIME & DISTANCE: At least 1.5 hours; about 25 miles.

GETTING THERE: You can go in either direction. I describe it going south. Take state Highway 62 east 14.2 miles from the turnoff to the park at Twentynine Palms. Turn right (south) onto Gold Crown Road. If you'd rather go north, the Old Dale Road turnoff is 6.8 miles northeast of Cottonwood Visitor Center.

THE DRIVE: Set your odometer at 0 when you turn off Highway 62. This is the location of Old Dale, a mining camp that sprouted after gold was discovered in the region in the early 1880s. (There are two more Dales to come.) Gold Crown Road is a good, wide dirt road. Follow it a bit more than 4.5 miles to Virginia Dale Mine, east of the road. It was founded in 1885. A second Dale grew up around this mine. In the early 1900s a gold discovery at the site of Supply Mine, 2 miles east, prompted folks to relocate the town. This third Dale, named New Dale, was located east of the main road where it turns sharply southwest. In a bit more than 2 miles the route goes left (southeast). Drive about 4 miles up into the Pinto Mountains, passing old mine sites, rubbish and private residences. The one-lane road, which becomes Old Dale Road, is rough in spots. Soon you'll begin the beautiful descent into Pinto Basin, in the park. You'll cross an ecological transition zone as you leave the Mojave Desert behind and enter the Colorado Desert. The vista is stunning in late afternoon's golden light and shadows. A half mile before the dirt road widens, you'll pass the remains of Mission Well on the right. The well provided water to local mines and mills in the 1930s. It's 9 miles to the paved road.

REST STOPS: Twentynine Palms. The historic sites. Note: Old mine sites are dangerous. In the park, it's illegal to take or remove anything, or to drive off designated roads.

GETTING HOME: Hwy. 62 west toward I-10.

MAPS: BLM's Chuckwalla and Sheephole Mountains maps. The park's brochure.

INFORMATION: Visitor centers at Twentynine Palms & Cottonwood; call the park at 619-367-7511.

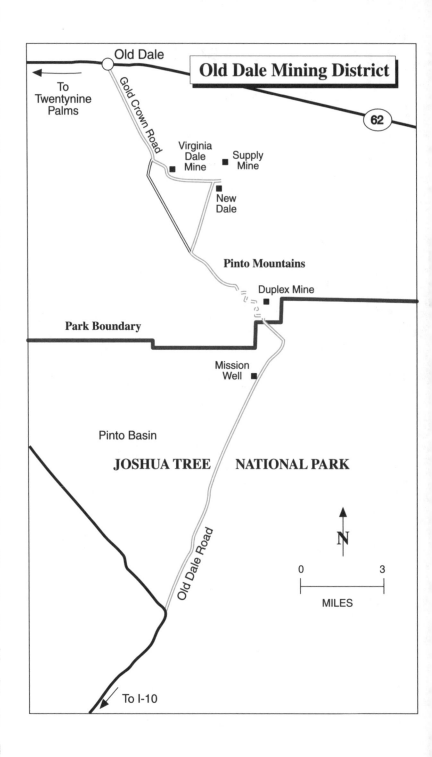

Old Dale

Old Dale Mining District

To Twentynine Palms

Gold Crown Road

62

Virginia Dale Mine

Supply Mine

New Dale

Pinto Mountains

Duplex Mine

Park Boundary

Mission Well

Pinto Basin

JOSHUA TREE   NATIONAL PARK

N

0   3

MILES

Old Dale Road

To I-10

Pinkham Canyon

LOCATION: Joshua Tree National Park, north of Interstate 10.

HIGHLIGHTS: Lush desert vegetation and a pretty canyon.

DIFFICULTY: Easy, but there are sandy and rocky stretches. At times the route can be confusing.

TIME & DISTANCE: 2.5 hours; 23 miles.

GETTING THERE: Begins across the road from the Cottonwood Spring Visitor Center.

THE DRIVE: Note: The road numbers referred to are the old BLM numbers shown on the BLM's Desert Access Guide. Since this area was transferred from the BLM to the National Park Service late in 1994, a different road number may appear on newer maps. You'll see the road and sign across from the visitor center. Set your odometer at 0. You'll be surprised at how lush and diverse the desert vegetation is along this drive on road J341, which is an easy two-track with a few rocky stretches. By 8 miles you'll enter the Cottonwood Mountains and the canyon, formed at first by low hills and some rock cliffs. At 12.5 miles things become a bit confusing. You'll be facing toward a hillside. Keep left. There might be a signpost, but in any case you want to continue south, down the canyon. At 13 miles you're in the rock canyon, and the route is going to get sandy, but since you're headed downhill it should be easy. By 18.3 miles you'll be on solid ground again, and then you'll cross rocky Pinkham Wash with lots of ocotillo and a cholla cactus garden (don't touch). The latter look soft, but they're treacherous. Soon you can see Interstate 10 up ahead, and the Cactus City rest area. You won't be able to exit there, unfortunately. Keep left at just over 19.1 miles, and soon you'll reach a hard–packed dirt service road. Go left, paralleling the freeway more or less for several miles. You'll come out at a paved road and freeway underpass. If you want to return to the park, it's about 6.5 miles east via I-10.

REST STOPS: No place in particular, except for the small visitor center.

GETTING HOME: I-10 east or west.

MAPS: BLM's Chuckwalla Desert Access Guide, or the park map.

INFORMATION: Joshua Tree National Park, 619-367-7511.

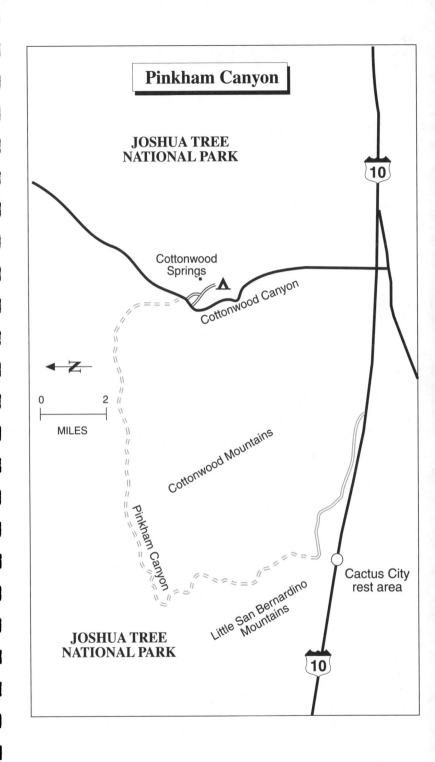

Painted Canyon

LOCATION: Southeast of Indio, in the Mecca Hills, between Interstate 10 and state Highway 111.

HIGHLIGHTS: Spectacular high-walled, narrow canyon with even narrower side canyons to explore. One of the most beautiful desert badlands canyons I've seen outside of Utah's canyon country. Bring plenty of medium-speed color film.

DIFFICULTY: Easy. But Riverside County may stop maintaining the road. If it does, the road's condition will deteriorate.

TIME & DISTANCE: 1 to 2 hours, depending on how much time you spend exploring; about 13 miles.

GETTING THERE: As you enter Mecca, on state Hwy. 111 southeast of Indio, veer right onto 66th Ave. The road, state Hwy. 195, will curve left, heading east through orchards and vineyards on a long straightaway. Go about 4.9 miles, pass the dump on the right, cross the Coachella Canal, then turn left onto Box Canyon Road at the sign for Painted Canyon. You'll be on road SR1711.

THE DRIVE: Following the graded dirt road, you'll soon see layered, folded and intricately eroded red and gray mountains. In the hills is a 41,300-acre recreation area that is largely the Mecca Hills Wilderness Area, where mechanized travel is not allowed. The road up Painted Canyon, located on the infamous San Andreas Fault, is an open route through this area. The geology here is busy indeed, and you'll be amazed by the folding, uplifting and faulting of these mudstone hills. By 3 miles you're in the canyon. Stop along the way. Get close to those powerful forces that are simultaneously building and tearing these sedimentary mountains down. The road ends at mile 4.7. Hike into the narrows up ahead, northeastward, to some ladders that help you through narrows. Or walk up the gorgeous, larger high-walled side canyon on the right. (Note the wilderness boundary marker. No motorized vehicles are allowed.) It ends in a mile at a beautiful dried waterfall basin.

REST STOPS: Picnic in the canyon. Visit the Palm Springs Desert Museum, Lake Cahuilla County Park, Living Desert, Santa Rosa Mountains National Scenic Area.

GETTING HOME: Retrace your route.

MAPS: BLM's Palm Springs, Chuckwalla Desert Guides.

INFORMATION: BLM Palm Springs/South Coast Resource Area Office, 619-251-4800.

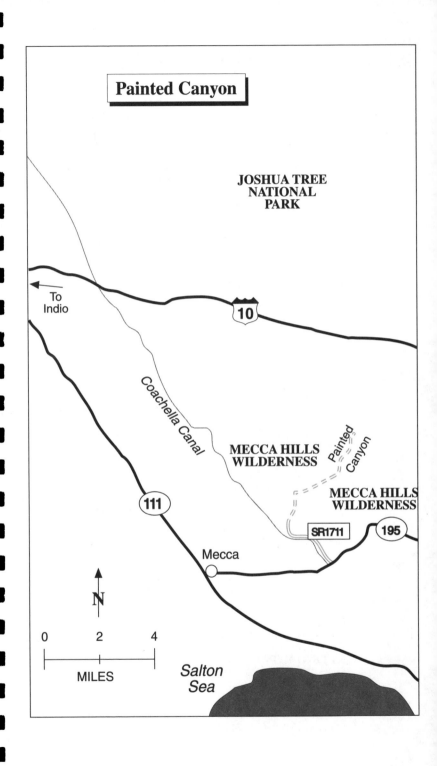

Painted Canyon

JOSHUA TREE
NATIONAL
PARK

To
Indio

10

Coachella Canal

MECCA HILLS
WILDERNESS

Painted Canyon

MECCA HILLS
WILDERNESS

SR1711

195

111

Mecca

N

0   2   4

MILES

Salton
Sea

Red Cloud Canyon

LOCATION: South of Interstate 10 in the Chuckwalla Mountains. About 40 miles east of Indio, and 9 miles west of Chiriaco Summit on I-10.

HIGHLIGHTS: A convenient adventure if you're weary of I–10. A fascinating, beautiful canyon in the Chuckwalla Mountains Wilderness. Old gold mines. Soaring raptors.

DIFFICULTY: Easy, but rocky in places.

TIME & DISTANCE: 1.5 hours; about 19 miles. Can be done as a side trip to the historic Bradshaw Trail, described separately.

GETTING THERE: From I-10, take the Red Cloud Road exit. Go 2.1 miles southeast, much of it beside railroad tracks, to a fork. The right branch, road C041, will take you to the Bradshaw Trail. The left fork is the Red Cloud Mine Road, C032. Take it, and set your odometer at 0.

THE DRIVE: You'll be driving on a designated route through the Chuckwalla Mountains Wilderness, where mechanized travel is restricted to designated roads. This road will take you southeast up Red Cloud Wash to a gorgeous canyon of marbled red and gray rock. It can get pretty bumpy. At 2.9 miles, where the road becomes rocky, you'll come to a fork; keep right. Do the same at the fork at 3.7 miles. There are some spurs off the main track, to the right, but stay on the main track. It's not hard to follow. You'll cross a broad, long area of desert pavement, or flat, broken, varnished rock. Notice the cholla cacti (don't touch!) and ocotillo. You'll cross a couple of easy washes, then follow the main canyon wash. At 7.3 miles you'll come to some mine ruins. Turn around here. This is Red Cloud Mine. Remember, it is illegal to deface or remove historic or cultural artifacts.

REST STOPS: Almost anywhere along the way. There are many primitive camp sites. The kids will love the old Army tanks at the General Patton Memorial Museum at Chiriaco Summit, on I-10. (The general's tank corps trained in this vast, inhospitable region.)

GETTING HOME: I-10.

MAP: BLM's Chuckwalla Desert Access Guide.

INFORMATION: BLM's Palm Springs/South Coast Recreation Area, 619-251-4800.

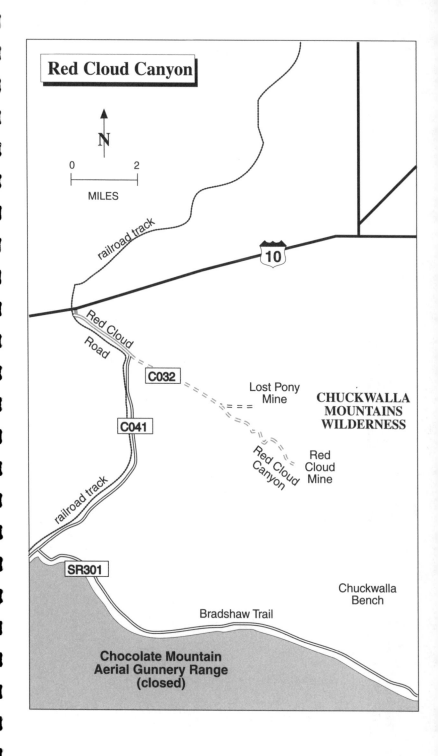

Red Cloud Canyon

Corn Springs

LOCATION: South of Interstate 10 in the Chuckwalla Mountains.

HIGHLIGHTS: Lovely oasis with huge native California fan palms, a campground, fine petroglyphs, lots of cacti and ocotillo. Dramatic desert mountain scenery.

DIFFICULTY: Easy, with one short moderate pitch.

TIME & DISTANCE: 2 hours; about 26 miles.

GETTING THERE: Take I-10 about 9.5 miles east of Desert Center. Take the Corn Springs Road exit; go right, then left onto Chuckwalla Road. In half a mile turn right (southwest) onto dirt and gravel Corn Springs Road.

THE DRIVE: Drive almost 7 miles from Chuckwalla Road, and suddenly, after you round a bend, there's a startling view of a grove of tall native palms. This area used to have reliable water, but the BLM says recent earthquakes apparently have reduced or terminated the underground water supply. The palms are suffering, evidenced by the shortening of their fronds from the typical 8-foot length to four or five feet. Just before you reach the campground you'll see on your right one of the finest displays of aboriginal rock art in the California Desert. According to the sign, they may date from 1000 B.C. to 1800 A.D. Veer left at the campground, past a self-guided nature trail. Continue west on the dirt and gravel road for about 3 miles. You're driving up Corn Springs Wash, a flat covered with so-called desert pavement. You'll come to a handful of residences at Aztec Well. Take the 4x4 spur that angles up to the right. It's just a short stretch that isn't as bad as it looks. It's road C061. Notice how relatively lush and diverse the vegetation is. It includes ocotillo that can be green even in summer if there's been enough rain, plus cholla and barrel cacti. About 2.5 miles from Aztec Well you'll come to a flat and open spot at the base of a hill. Take a break here, then retrace your route.

REST STOPS: The fee campground has toilets, water, shaded tables. Explore the Chuckwalla Mountains Wilderness afoot. (No mechanized travel is allowed.)

GETTING HOME: Return to I-10.

MAP: BLM's Chuckwalla Desert Access Guide.

INFORMATION: BLM Palm Springs/South Coast Resource Area, 619-251-4800. Talk to the campground host.

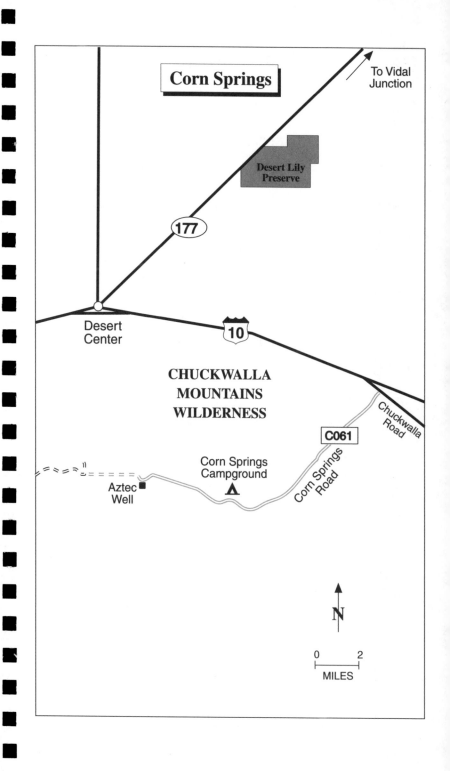

Corn Springs

To Vidal
Junction

Desert Lily
Preserve

177

Desert
Center

10

CHUCKWALLA
MOUNTAINS
WILDERNESS

C061

Chuckwalla
Road

Corn Springs
Campground

Corn Springs Road

Aztec
Well

N

0   2
MILES

Bradshaw Trail

LOCATION: South of Interstate 10 between the Chuckwalla Mountains and the Chocolate Mt. Aerial Gunnery Range.

HIGHLIGHTS: Between 1862 and 1877 this historic road was western California's primary route to and from the gold mines at La Paz, Ariz., along the Colorado River. It extended between Dos Palmas, on the Salton Sea, to the Colorado River. Established by William Bradshaw, it is today a BLM Back Country Byway. If you have the time, it's a great alternative to I-10. It crosses the Chuckwalla Bench, a premier example in California of a diverse Colorado Desert plant community that includes the rare and huge Munz cholla cactus.

DIFFICULTY: Easy. Don't drive in the gunnery range, or Chuckwalla Mountains Wilderness.

TIME & DISTANCE: 3.5 hours; about 60 miles.

GETTING THERE: If you're eastbound on I-10, take the Red Cloud Road exit about 40 miles east of Indio. Go southwest. If you're westbound, you can take the Chuckwalla Road exit, and turn south after about 2.9 miles onto road C081 to Graham Pass. Or take the Corn Springs exit, do that drive, then go about 12 miles southeast on the Chuckwalla Road and turn south on road C081 toward Graham Pass. I describe it from the Red Cloud Road exit.

THE DRIVE: You might have some company in the form of military aircraft. At the bottom of the exit, straight ahead, is road C032. Take it; set your odometer at 0. After 2.1 miles you'll reach road C041, the road you'll take. C032 goes left to Red Cloud Canyon, described separately. Continue south along the railroad tracks on road CO41. At 10.4 miles you'll reach the left (east) turn onto SR301, the Bradshaw Trail. You'll cross alluvial fans, washes and expanses of desert pavement. By about 45 miles, shortly before the left (north) turn onto road C081 to Graham Pass, go right onto Indian Well Road. You'll soon see the big Munz chollas. Take the road over 1,600-foot Graham Pass, and descend to Chuckwalla Road. I-10 is 2.9 miles to the right. Or go about 12 miles to the left to the Corn Springs turnoff near the freeway.

REST STOPS: Primitive campsites. The General Patton Memorial Museum at Chiriaco Summit on I-10.

GETTING HOME: I-10 east or west.

MAPS: Chuckwalla & Salton Sea Desert Access Guides.

INFORMATION: BLM's Palms Springs/South Coast Resource Area, 619-251-4800.

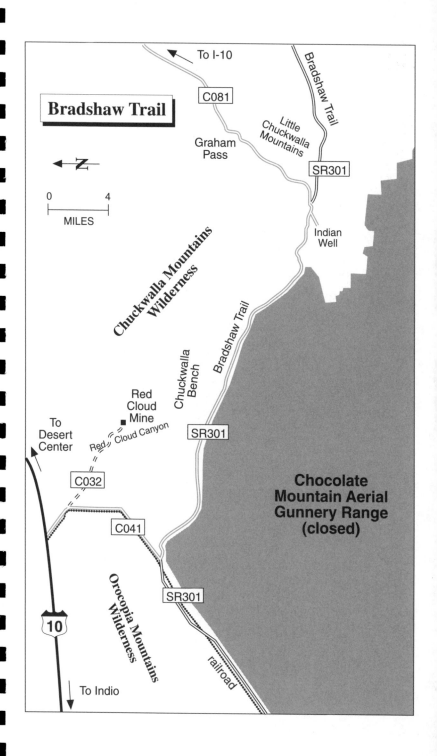

Bradshaw Trail

To I-10

Bradshaw Trail

C081

Little Chuckwalla Mountains

Graham Pass

SR301

N

0   4
MILES

Indian Well

Chuckwalla Mountains Wilderness

Bradshaw Trail

Chuckwalla Bench

Red Cloud Mine

To Desert Center

Red Cloud Canyon

SR301

C032

Chocolate Mountain Aerial Gunnery Range (closed)

C041

Orocopia Mountains Wilderness

SR301

10

railroad

To Indio

Font's Point

LOCATION: Anza-Borrego Desert State Park

HIGHLIGHTS: Outstanding vista across the Borrego Badlands to northern Mexico.

DIFFICULTY: Easy. But conditions in the sandy wash you'll drive up do change.

TIME & DISTANCE: An hour or less; 7.8 miles round-trip.

GETTING THERE: The turnoff is 3.7 miles east of where road S22 makes a sharp bend to the east; or 8.8 miles from the intersection of Borrego Valley Road and Palm Canyon Drive. Turn south at the sign.

THE DRIVE: Drive directly up Font's Point Wash. If you've never driven up a desert wash, and want a taste of what it's like, this is a fine introduction. At the point, you'll have a truly spectacular view of the colorful, deeply eroded badlands. These uplifted sediments range in age from 250,000 to 4 million years old. In addition to the badlands, you'll see Borrego Valley, the Salton Sea, Baja California, the Vallecito Mountains, Split Mountain and other sights. The point is named for Father Pedro Font, the diarist and chaplain during Spanish explorer Juan Bautista de Anza's second journey through this forbidding place in 1775-1776, when he led 240 settlers and soldiers to San Francisco Bay.

REST STOPS: You won't need one on this short drive.

GETTING HOME: Return the way you came.

MAPS: Park map; or BLM's McCain Valley Desert Access Guide.

INFORMATION: Call the park at 619-767-4205. For spring wildflower information, call 619-767-4684.

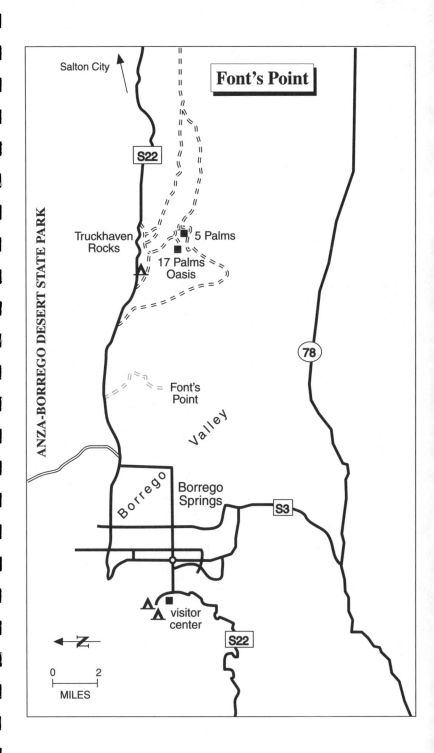

Font's Point

Salton City

S22

Truckhaven Rocks

5 Palms

17 Palms Oasis

ANZA-BORREGO DESERT STATE PARK

78

Font's Point

Valley

Borrego

Borrego Springs

S3

visitor center

S22

N

0   2
MILES

Seventeen Palms

LOCATION: Eastern Anza-Borrego Desert State Park.

HIGHLIGHTS: A fun drive down washes, ending at a historic palm oasis.

DIFFICULTY: Easy.

TIME & DISTANCE: An hour; 7.6 miles round-trip.

GETTING THERE: From Christmas Circle in Borrego Springs, take road S22 15.7 miles, then turn right onto a wash. You'll see a sign stating "Arroyo Salado" on the right, and a nearby signpost for the 17 Palms trail.

THE DRIVE: Drive up Arroyo Salado for about 3.8 miles. Veer right. In a short distance you'll come to a parking area with a stone monument explaining the historic significance of this verdant oasis. You'll see the grove of native palms nearby, looking just like the oases in those old French Foreign Legion movies. You will be the latest visitors in a stream of humans who've been drawn here for thousands of years. Nomadic aboriginal people, emigrants and prospectors have all come to this island in the badlands for water, shade and rest. The oasis is a remnant of an era when grasslands, streams, camels and mammoths shared a very different world. The palms are sustained by surface water here. The spring is unreliable, so early travelers would leave water for others in large glass jars in the shade. (The spring's water is not potable, by the way, so don't drink it.) They'd also leave written messages in this "prospector's post office." The tradition continues; check the middle palms for water jugs and daily diaries. You'll see that people from all over the world come here. The Font's Point drive, described separately, is 5.4 miles west of where you left the highway.

REST STOPS: The oasis itself. Borrego Springs has all services, including some exclusive resorts with golf courses, tennis courts, restaurants and other amenities.

GETTING HOME: Back on S22, go left to return to Borrego Springs, or right to Salton City.

MAPS: Park map, or the BLM's McCain Valley Desert Access Guide.

INFORMATION: Stop at the park visitor center at Borrego Springs. Or call the park at 619-767-4205. For spring wildflower information, call 619-767-4684.

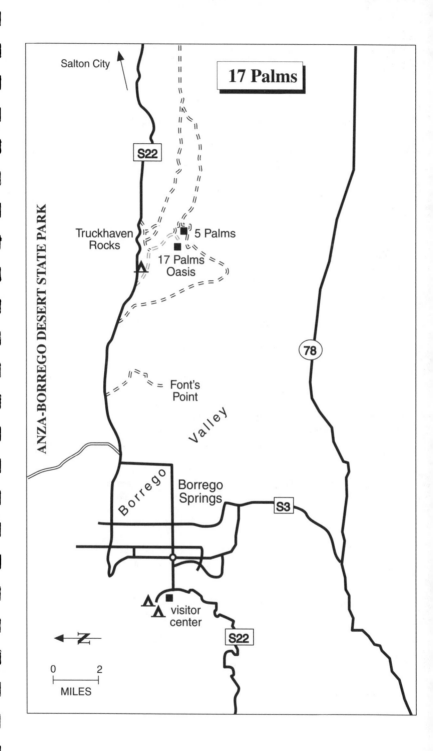

17 Palms

Salton City

S22

ANZA-BORREGO DESERT STATE PARK

Truckhaven Rocks

5 Palms

17 Palms Oasis

78

Font's Point

Valley

Borrego

Borrego Springs

S3

visitor center

S22

N

0   2

MILES

Old Culp Valley Road

LOCATION: Western Anza-Borrego Desert State Park.

HIGHLIGHTS: A pretty drive through mountains with relatively lush desert vegetation. Nice views.

DIFFICULTY: Easy.

TIME & DISTANCE: An hour; 5.5 miles.

GETTING THERE: From Borrego Springs, take road S22 west up the steep grade for about 11.5 miles. It begins 0.4 mile west of the park entrance. Turn left (south) onto the two-track road running parallel to Wilson Road, and set your odometer at 0.

THE DRIVE: You're at almost 4,000 feet elevation at the start, crossing through a rich variety of surprisingly lush vegetation, while the arid Borrego Valley below and to the east lies at about 450 feet above sea level. You'll have a very pretty descent into little Culp Valley, which lies at about 2,800 feet. Start by crossing a grassy meadow, and at 0.7 mile from the highway take a hard left. In about half a mile you'll reach an intersection. To the right is the Jasper Trail. Continue straight. After about 4.9 miles you'll pass a road to the right, which goes a short distance to a picnic area at the old Paroli home site. Soon you'll enter a meadow surrounded by boulder-strewn hills, and then you'll reach paved S22. Borrego Springs is right, back down the grade.

REST STOPS: Borrego Springs has all services, and some very upscale resorts. The Culp Valley Primitive Camp Area.

GETTING HOME: Return the way you came.

MAP: This road is difficult to see on the BLM's McCain Valley Desert Access Guide. It is shown on the park's map.

INFORMATION: Stop at the park visitor center at Borrego Springs. Or call the park at 619-767-4205. For spring wildflower information, call 619-767-4684. If you send them a stamped, self-addressed postcard, they'll mail it to you when the flowers bloom. See the addresses in the back of the book.

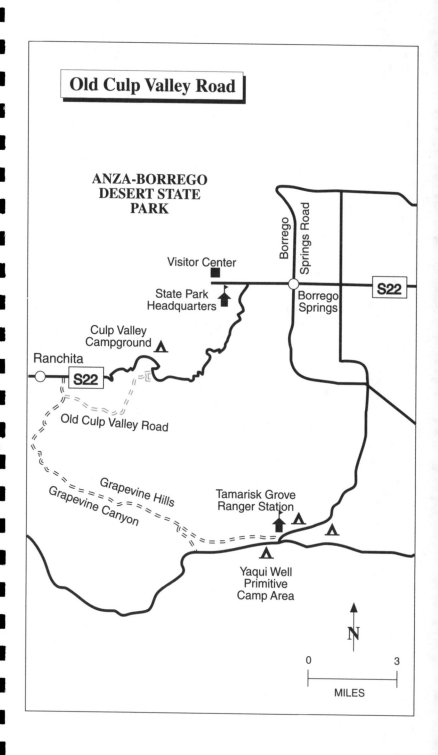

Old Culp Valley Road

ANZA-BORREGO
DESERT STATE
PARK

Visitor Center

State Park
Headquarters

Borrego Springs Road

Borrego Springs

S22

Culp Valley
Campground

Ranchita

S22

Old Culp Valley Road

Grapevine Hills

Grapevine Canyon

Tamarisk Grove
Ranger Station

Yaqui Well
Primitive
Camp Area

N

0   3
MILES

Grapevine Canyon

LOCATION: Western Anza-Borrego Desert State Park.

HIGHLIGHTS: Fine views and changing desert vegetation as you drop from almost 4,000 feet elevation to about 1,400 feet.

DIFFICULTY: Easy, with a few short stretches of sand and rough road surface.

TIME & DISTANCE: 1.5 hours; 13 miles.

GETTING THERE: From Borrego Springs, take road S22 west up the steep grade for about 11.5 miles. Turn left (south) 0.4 mile west of the park entrance onto Wilson Road. Set your odometer at 0 here. You'll pass private residences on this drive, so drive slowly and be considerate.

THE DRIVE: You'll pass several side routes as you drive into the Grapevine Hills to Grapevine Canyon. After about 2.75 miles, when you descend into the canyon, you'll come to a T intersection. Go left, or southeast. Signs along the way will let you know that the people who live here take privacy and safe driving seriously. After about 4 miles you'll pass Grapevine Springs Ranch and Vineyards, and then you'll cross into the park, following some power lines. There will be a short stretch of slight and easy sand. At 4.7 miles you'll see wild grapevines on the left. About 1.3 miles from that point, there's a tricky little intersection. Look for a post, and go around it and to the left. The road will be more adventurous from here as you descend along the side of the canyon. At about 8.7 miles from the start you'll reach a right turn to Highway 78. But continue on through Yaqui Flat to road S3. The Tamarisk Grove Ranger Station is to your left.

REST STOPS: Culp Valley Primitive Camp Area on the way to the starting point. Or at the end, the Yaqui Well Primitive Camp Area, Tamarisk Grove Campground, or the Yaqui Pass Primitive Camp Area. Borrego Springs has all services, including some very upscale resorts.

GETTING HOME: You'll come out at state Highway 78. Escondido is west, Brawley is east, or go north on S3 to Borrego Springs.

MAPS: Park map; the BLM's McCain Valley Desert Guide.

INFORMATION: Stop at the Tamarisk Grove Ranger Station or the park visitor center at Borrego Springs. Or call the park at 619-767-4205. For spring wildflower information call 619-767-4684.

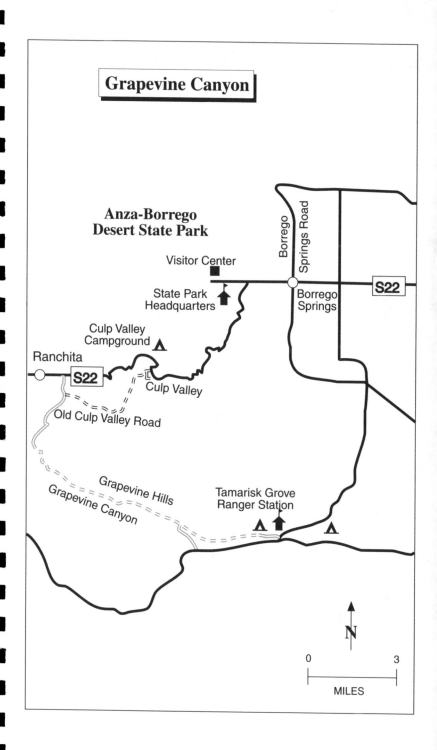

Grapevine Canyon

Anza-Borrego Desert State Park

Visitor Center

State Park Headquarters

Borrego Springs Road

Borrego Springs

S22

Culp Valley Campground

Ranchita

S22

Culp Valley

Old Culp Valley Road

Grapevine Hills

Grapevine Canyon

Tamarisk Grove Ranger Station

N

0   3

MILES

Indian Pass

LOCATION: North of Yuma, Ariz.; just west of Picacho State Recreation Area in the Chocolate Mountains.

HIGHLIGHTS: Gorgeous low-desert scenery along the Colorado River. Wildlife.

DIFFICULTY: Easy to moderate. There's a narrow, rocky, eroded stretch of road on the descent from the pass to sandy Gavilan Wash. The segment along the river can be flooded in periods of high water, so check with Picacho State Recreation Area before setting out.

TIME & DISTANCE: 2.5 hours; 23 miles from Ogilby Road to Picacho.

GETTING THERE: From the south, take Interstate 8 east beyond the vast Imperial Sand Dunes. Turn north on Ogilby Road (Imperial County Road S34) and go 13.1 miles. Turn east (right) on Indian Pass Road (A272). From the north, take state Highway 78 to S34, then south 10.4 miles to Indian Pass Road.

THE DRIVE: This can be taken in either direction, but whenever a drive involves sand I recommend the downhill direction. So I describe it going west to east. The graded dirt road crosses a broad, open region heading toward a tall rock fin on the horizon, passing ocotillo, cholla cactus and creosote. You'll pass numerous sandy washes lined with palo verde and ironwood trees. Rock hounds will like the area. Spring wildflowers can be profuse after a wet winter. After 6 miles you'll see the road heading toward a gap in the hills, and jagged peaks beyond the gap. That's Indian Pass. The half-mile descent to Gavilan Wash is narrow, rocky and eroded, deserving a moderate rating. Go right when you reach the wash, staying on the main tracks for the next 6.2 miles to a fork. The sign will indicate that 4–S Ranch, actually a boat ramp and primitive camping area, is left. You can go that way and explore. The main route goes right, and for the next 7.6 miles you'll have an exotic drive along the Colorado River to Picacho.

REST STOPS: Lots of good primitive camping along Indian Pass Road, and developed sites in the recreation area along the river. Stop at the Gold Rock Trading Post on Gold Rock Ranch Road, and the nearby old town site of Tumco.

GETTING HOME: Picacho Road (A481) south to Imperial County Road S24, then Interstate 8.

MAP: BLM's Midway Well Desert Access Guide.

INFORMATION: Picacho SRA, 619-996-2963; BLM El Centro Resource Area, 619-337-4400.

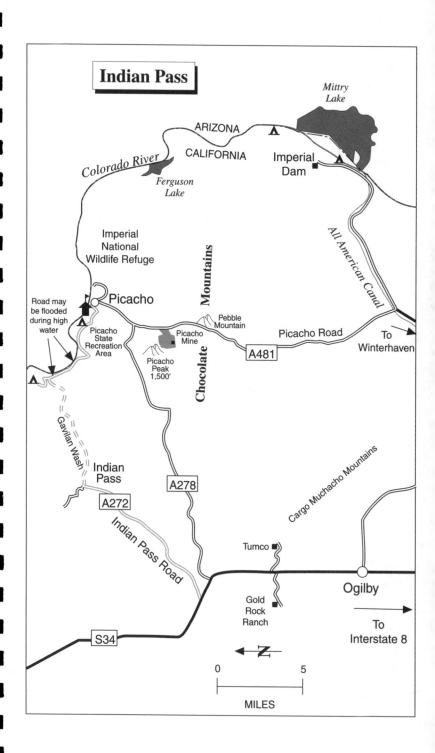

Indian Pass

Mittry Lake

ARIZONA

CALIFORNIA

Colorado River

Ferguson Lake

Imperial Dam

All American Canal

Imperial National Wildlife Refuge

Picacho

Pebble Mountain

Picacho Road

A481

To Winterhaven

Road may be flooded during high water

Picacho State Recreation Area

Picacho Mine

Picacho Peak 1,500'

Chocolate Mountains

Gavilan Wash

Indian Pass

A272

A278

Indian Pass Road

Cargo Muchacho Mountains

Tumco

Ogilby

Gold Rock Ranch

To Interstate 8

S34

N

0   5

MILES

Picacho Road

LOCATION: In the Chocolate Mountains north of Yuma, Ariz; Picacho State Recreation Area.

HIGHLIGHTS: Outstanding multicolored desert scenery, reminiscent of Utah's canyon country. Ends at the Colorado River. Includes a spur to a spectacular overlook.

DIFFICULTY: Easy.

TIME & DISTANCE: 3 to 4 hours, or you can camp overnight; about 50 miles round-trip including the excellent river overlook spur.

GETTING THERE: From Interstate 8 at Winterhaven, take the Fourth Avenue exit, which connects to Imperial County Road S24. Where S24 curves sharply right (east), go straight (north) to Picacho Road (A481). Soon the pavement will end. Set your odometer at 0.

THE DRIVE: The first 14 miles or so are boring on a good, wide graded road as you cross a flat. Then the road narrows and begins to wind through an area of eroded hills and washes. Suddenly, at 16.4 miles, a vast and primeval vista of carved canyons and small ranges appears. Notice the fin, a tall but narrow slice of rock, on the left. You'll pass the Picacho Mine, a gold mine. By 21.6 miles you'll enter the 7,000-acre state recreation area. It costs $5 to drive through. This is an old mining region. The town of Picacho was located where the campground is now. At the turn of the century it had 2,500 people. Just beyond the SRA entrance, a small road goes to the right. It's Railroad Canyon Road, a wonderful 4-mile spur, round–trip, that follows a turn-of-the-century railroad bed to a fabulous overlook. The road ends where there used to be a railroad trestle. Until 1906 trains hauled ore to mills along the river below. Back at the park entrance, go right to the river, where you'll find a boat launch, sheltered tables, water and toilets. Steamboats serviced a port here until 1910. It eventually became a squatters' haven. The park office is a cabin left over from squatters who once lived here. The area became a state recreation area in 1961.

REST STOPS: There are developed campgrounds. There's a shady picnic table along the overlook spur. Yuma has all services.

GETTING HOME: Retrace your route.

MAP: BLM's Midway Well Desert Access Guide.

INFORMATION: Picacho SRA, 619-393-3052.

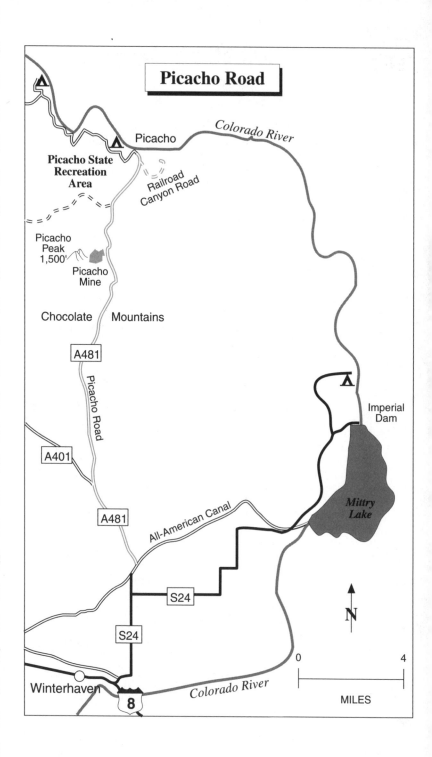

Picacho Road

Sandstone Canyon

LOCATION: Anza-Borrego Desert State Park.

HIGHLIGHTS: If you only do one drive in the park, do this one. It has it all: an outstanding scenic and geologic experience, strange wind caves, a primeval landscape, and a very narrow, deep, colorful canyon at the end with walls 200 feet high. Before you reach Split Mountain there is a hiking side trip to some elephant trees. Spring wildflowers.

DIFFICULTY: Easy, but if you drive into Sandstone Canyon you'll find turning around to be very tricky. Instead, park at the canyon's entrance and walk.

TIME & DISTANCE: At least half a day; 36 miles.

GETTING THERE: Take state Highway 78 to Ocotillo Wells. Go south on Split Mountain Road. At 5.8 miles from the highway take a right to the 1.5-mile, 1 hour Elephant Trees Trail. About 2.1 miles farther you'll reach Fish Creek Wash. Set your odometer at 0. Go right, up the wash.

THE DRIVE: You'll head up a wide wash toward the split in Split Mountain, which was carved by powerful floods cutting through rising mountains. The action has exposed colorful red walls, cobbles and, at 3.6 miles, fascinating pressure bends, or anticline, in the canyon's sandstone wall on the right. The split separates the Vallecito Mountains on the right (west) and Fish Creek Mountains on the left (east). Continuing through the canyon, you'll come out into the Carrizo Badlands. At 4.2 miles, on the left, is the trailhead for the vigorous, 20–minute hike up to the wind caves, huge eroded, honeycombed rocks. The view from them of the badlands, including the hills dubbed Fossil Shelf, is fantastic. The dark brown crust on the hilltops is fossilized mollusks. You'll drive along the base of sandstone cliffs on your right. At 6.8 miles you'll pass Loop Wash on the right. At 8 miles, at a Y, go either way. By about 12.4 miles you'll see a sign on the left for Sandstone Canyon, a slit in the rock cliffs. In about 1.5 miles you'll reach a boulder that leaves only enough room for a small vehicle to pass. But there's a rockfall 0.1 mile farther, so walk from here or turn back.

REST STOPS: Fish Creek Primitive C.G.; anywhere else.

GETTING HOME: Return to Ocotillo Wells; right to state Highway 86 and Salton City, left to Borrego Springs.

MAPS: Park map; BLM McCain Valley Guide.

INFORMATION: The visitor center at Borrego Springs. Or call 619-767-4205. For wildflower news, call 619-767-4684.

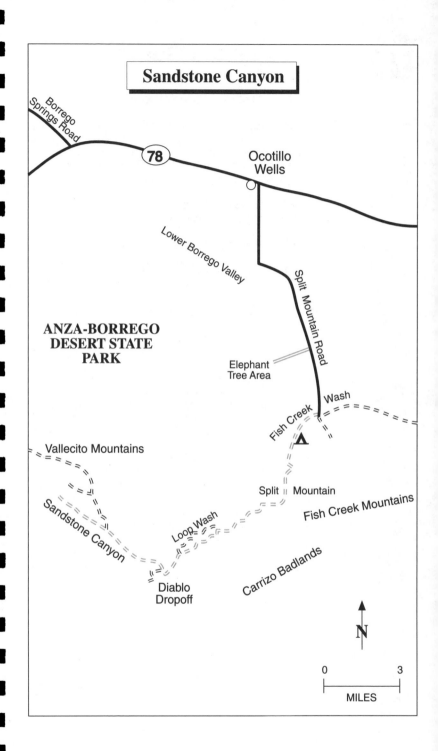

Sandstone Canyon

Borrego Springs Road

78

Ocotillo Wells

Lower Borrego Valley

ANZA-BORREGO DESERT STATE PARK

Split Mountain Road

Elephant Tree Area

Fish Creek Wash

Vallecito Mountains

Split Mountain

Loop Wash

Fish Creek Mountains

Sandstone Canyon

Diablo Dropoff

Carrizo Badlands

N

0   3
MILES

Painted Gorge

LOCATION: North of Ocotillo, off Interstate 8.

HIGHLIGHTS: An intriguing, narrow gorge of colorful rock in the area of an ancient lake. A great side trip to break up a long freeway journey. Also in this region are the Fossil Canyon, Yuha Basin and Smuggler's Cave drives that are described in the next few pages.

DIFFICULTY: Moderate. There is one very narrow spot to carefully creep through, and some rocky stretches.

TIME & DISTANCE: 1.5 to 2 hours; 14.7 miles round-trip.

GETTING THERE: From I-8, take the Ocotillo/Imperial Highway exit. Go east on Imperial County Road S80, and in about 4.2 miles you'll see a sign for the turnoff (left, or north) onto road Y181 to Painted Gorge. Set your odometer at 0.

THE DRIVE: Painted Gorge is surrounded by the newly designated Coyote Mountains Wilderness. Not far to the north are a number of military bombing areas. To the south is the protected Jacumba Wilderness. Such is the irony of the California Desert. Anyway, after 1.4 miles you'll reach a Y, pass some residences and enter the seemingly barren Coyote Mountains. At 3.5 miles you'll reach a gravel pit; drive through it, and you'll find the road on the other side. Keep right at the Y at 4.4 miles. At 4.7 miles is yet another Y. An arrow, formed of rocks on the ground, points left, but keep right. After another 0.2 mile you'll reach yet another Y, in a little bowl of yellow rock. Go left, between two bushes, drive up a wash and enter the narrow gorge of colored rocks. You'll eventually come to a point where the road makes a hard right, and climbs. That's a serious and rough 4x4 trail. Hike it, or turn around here.

REST STOPS: Look for fossils in the gorge's walls, whose colors stem from copper, sulfur and iron content. El Centro has all services. There's a park with playground equipment at North 6th and Park Avenue in El Centro. Try Sunbeam Lake County Park, west of El Centro.

GETTING HOME: I-8.

MAP: BLM's Imperial Valley South Desert Access Guide.

INFORMATION: BLM's El Centro Resource Area Office, 619-337-4400.

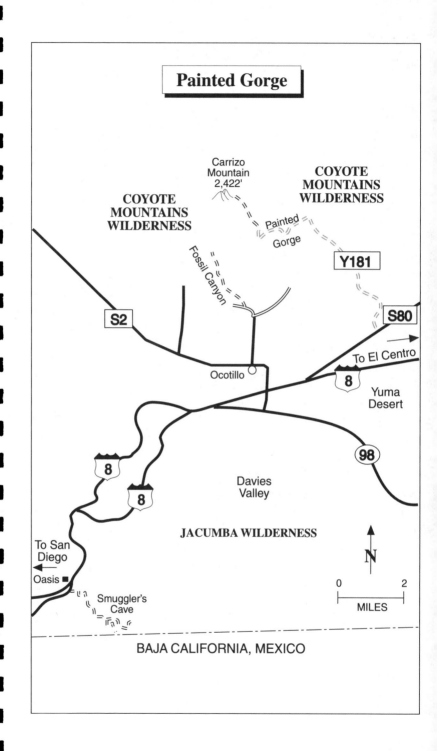

Painted Gorge

Carrizo Mountain 2,422'

COYOTE MOUNTAINS WILDERNESS

COYOTE MOUNTAINS WILDERNESS

Painted Gorge

Fossil Canyon

Y181

S2

S80

To El Centro

8

Ocotillo

Yuma Desert

8

8

98

Davies Valley

JACUMBA WILDERNESS

N

To San Diego

Oasis

Smuggler's Cave

0   2
MILES

BAJA CALIFORNIA, MEXICO

Fossil Canyon

LOCATION: North of Ocotillo, off Interstate 8.

HIGHLIGHTS: Another colorful, narrow canyon, and another opportunity to break up a long freeway trek by exploring a fascinating canyon with a 50-million-year geologic history. A great place to explore afoot as well. Also in this area are the Painted Gorge, Yuha Basin and Smuggler's Cave drives.

DIFFICULTY: Easy, but rocky and narrow in spots.

TIME & DISTANCE: 1.5 hours; 5.5 miles.

GETTING THERE: From I-8, take the Ocotillo/Imperial Highway exit. Follow Imperial County Road S2 through Ocotillo. At a stop sign shortly after the sharp bend to the left, go right (north) onto Shell Canyon Road. The pavement will end. The vague, unmarked right to Fossil Canyon is 0.15 mile after you pass beneath the power lines, as the main road makes a long westward bend. If you reach the gravel operation, you've missed it.

THE DRIVE: This canyon, like Painted Gorge, cuts through an area where an ancient lake once was located. It's not so narrow or rocky as Painted Gorge. The reddish-yellow layers of sedimentary rock, some vertical and some horizontal, were laid down when ancient lakes covered the area and, over the eons, were rearranged by geologic forces. Along the way you'll pass a small side canyon on the left. It's worth a short hike; don't drive up it. The driving ends at an opening in the rock wall ahead that looks like a natural gate of sorts. The newly designated Coyote Wilderness is to the north.

REST STOPS: No place special. Look for fossils in the canyon's walls. El Centro has all services.

GETTING HOME: Return to I-8.

MAP: BLM's Imperial Valley South Desert Access Guide.

INFORMATION: BLM's El Centro Resource Area Office, 619-337-4400.

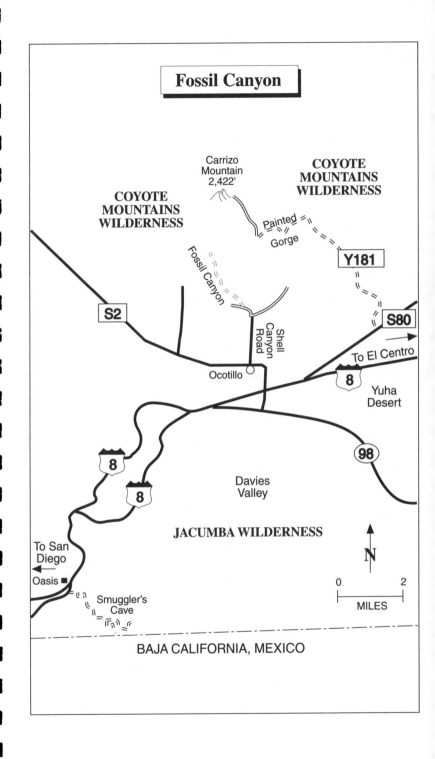

Fossil Canyon

Yuha Basin

LOCATION: About 100 miles east of San Diego, between state Highway 98 and Interstate 8.

HIGHLIGHTS: Yuha Well, where Capt. Juan Bautista de Anza, the Spanish explorer who established the first overland emigrant trail from Mexico, camped during two expeditions in the 1770s; oyster shell fossil beds, left over from Lake LeConte, which covered most of Imperial and central Riverside counties about 6 million years ago; Yuha geoglyph, a prehistoric symbol on the ground made by the Kamia Indians. Spring flowers.

DIFFICULTY: Easy; some sand. A confusing place, but the BLM is planning to put up more signs.

TIME & DISTANCE: About 1.5 to 2 hours; 12 miles, depending on how much exploring you do.

GETTING THERE: Exit I-8 at Ocotillo. Take Imperial County Road S2 right, or south, a short distance to state Highway 98. Go left (east) for 5.9 miles. Turn left (north) on road Y1928, which is dirt.

THE DRIVE: It's a strange area of low hills, badlands, flats and eroded washes. From the highway take Y1928 for 0.8 mile to a Y. Go straight (north), staying on Y1928. It will curve northeast along the western rim of the basin past a fenced geoglyph, which vandals badly damaged in 1975. About 4 miles from that first Y, a road to the right (southwest), Y1950, will take you in a bit more than a mile to the Yuha Well area, where Anza camped. Farther on, road Y1945 goes to the oyster shell fossil beds. The main route, now Y1950, continues northeast another 3.5 miles or so to I-8 and Dunaway Road. Note: To visit the overlook and monument to the explorer that is noted on your map, go right at that first Y, onto road Y2739, and in another 0.8 mile you'll reach it. The explorer's first small expedition, in 1774, crossed the forbidding desert basin below on its way from the Tubac region, in Arizona near Tucson, to Monterey. He led a far larger group, the founders of San Francisco, the next year.

REST STOPS: Ocotillo. In El Centro, there's a park with playground equipment at North 6th and Park Avenue.

GETTING HOME: I-8.

MAP: BLM's Imperial Valley South Desert Access Guide.

INFORMATION: BLM, El Centro, 619-337-4400.

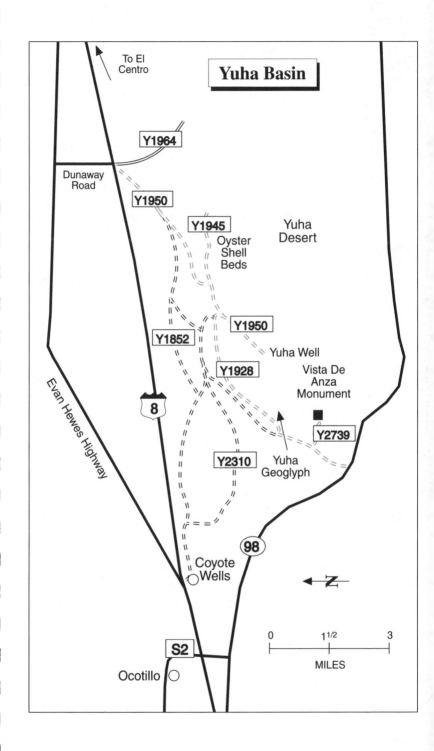

Smuggler's Cave

LOCATION: About 85 miles east of San Diego, just south of Interstate 8.

HIGHLIGHTS: A strange jumble of huge granite rocks very close to the Mexican border. They form bizarre piles and towers that create many mazes and caves. Fine views. Smuggler's Cave is a hollow in one of the boulders, said to have been used by miscreants in the late 1800s and early 1900s. Convenient for folks who need a break from I-8. Bring a mountain bike to tour the area, or hike. The Fossil Canyon, Painted Gorge and Yuha Basin drives described in this book are farther east on I-8.

DIFFICULTY: Moderate; one difficult spot.

TIME & DISTANCE: 1 to 1.5 hours, but it's worth taking more time to explore the intriguing landscape; about 4.5 miles round–trip.

GETTING THERE: From eastbound I-8 take the In-Ko-Pah Park Road exit near Oasis. Go right at the bottom of the exit, then right again on a paved road, and go almost 0.2 mile. Then turn left onto a dirt area, and immediately left again. That's the route, Y2219.

THE DRIVE: Follow the single-lane road up a steep hill, the steepest parts of which have been crudely paved. No doubt spinning tires must have caused a lot of damage before some asphalt was laid down. Keep left when you reach a fork. The right fork is very bad, and reconnects to the main route anyway in a short distance. You'll have some great views as you climb to about 3,700 feet above sea level. As you descend toward the rocks of the Smuggler's Cave area there is a very nasty, but short, rocky pitch. Use low range, and take it slow. (Coming back, I found it best to keep right at that spot, but things change. Plan your approach before you get there.) Not too much farther things will get too rough to continue, so find a good place to stop and turn around. Do some exploring on foot, or by mountain bike. A short distance farther south is the Mexican border. In those hills is the Elliott Mine, a small active gold mine.

REST STOPS: Explore the rocks or unload your mountain bike. Primitive camping.

GETTING HOME: I-8 east or west.

MAP: BLM's Imperial Valley South Desert Access Guide.

INFORMATION: BLM's El Centro Resource Area Office, 619-337-4400.

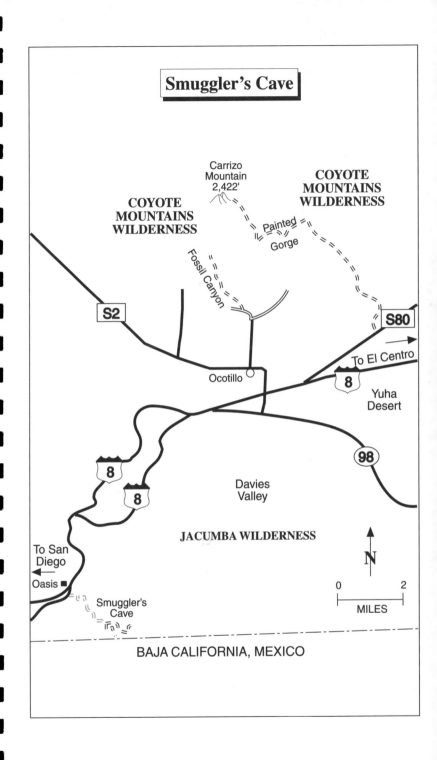

Smuggler's Cave

COYOTE MOUNTAINS WILDERNESS

Carrizo Mountain 2,422'

COYOTE MOUNTAINS WILDERNESS

Painted Gorge

Fossil Canyon

S2

S80

To El Centro

8

Ocotillo

Yuha Desert

98

8

8

Davies Valley

JACUMBA WILDERNESS

N

To San Diego

Oasis ■

Smuggler's Cave

0   2
MILES

BAJA CALIFORNIA, MEXICO

Trip notes

The Colorado River from Railroad Canyon Road, Picacho S.R.A.

APPENDIX

Automobile Club of Southern California maps

Trips & recommended maps:
1. Volcanic Tableland: Guide to Eastern Sierra
2. White Mountains Loop: Guide to Eastern Sierra
3. Owens Valley/Death Valley: Guide to Eastern Sierra & Guide to Death Valley
4. Inyo Mountains: Guide to Eastern Sierra (Omits the northern segment of the route, from Blue Bell Mine to the Big Pine-Death Valley Road. Also, it refers to Mazourka Peak as Barber Peak).
5. Saline Valley Road: Guide to Death Valley
6. The Racetrack: Guide to Death Valley
7. Cerro Gordo: Guide to Death Valley
8. Hidden Valley: Guide to Death Valley
9. Titus Canyon: Guide to Death Valley
10. Chloride City: Guide to Death Valley
11. Cottonwood/Marble canyons: Guide to Death Valley
12. Echo Canyon: Guide to Death Valley
13. Hole-In-The-Wall: Guide to Death Valley
14. Darwin Falls to Darwin: Guide to Death Valley
15. Butte Valley: Guide to Death Valley
16. Trona Pinnacles: San Bernardino County
17. Burro Schmidt's Tunnel: Kern County
18. Red Rock Canyon State Park: San Luis Obispo & Bakersfield to Los Angeles
19. Alphie Canyon: San Luis Obispo & Bakersfield to Los Angeles
20. Jawbone to Isabella Lake: Sequoia; Kern County
21. Inscription Canyon Loop: San Bernardino County
22. Cedar Canyon Road: San Bernardino County
23. Afton Canyon: San Bernardino County
24. Wild Horse Canyon: San Bernardino County
25. Ivanpah-Lanfair Road: San Bernardino County
26. Black Canyon Road: San Bernardino County
27. Mojave Road: San Bernardino County (only shows segments; Mojave Road isn't designated as such)
28. Stoddard Well Road: San Bernardino County
29. Rodman Mountains Loop: San Bernardino County
30. Camp Rock Road: San Bernardino County
31. Big Bear Road: San Bernardino County
32. Covington Flats: Riverside County
33. Geology Tour: Riverside County
34. Old Dale Mining District: Riverside County
35. Pinkham Canyon: Riverside County (omits southern segment, to I-10)
36. Painted Canyon: Riverside County
37. Red Cloud Canyon: Riverside County
38. Corn Springs: Riverside County
39. Bradshaw Trail: Riverside County
40. Font's Point: San Diego County
41. 17 Palms: San Diego County
42. Old Culp Valley Road: San Diego County
43. Grapevine Canyon: San Diego County
44. Indian Pass: Imperial County
45. Picacho Road: Imperial County
46. Sandstone Canyon: San Diego County
47. Painted Gorge: Imperial County
48. Fossil Canyon: Imperial County
49. Yuha Basin: Imperial County
50. Smuggler's Cave: San Diego County

Information

NOTE: Most of the telephone numbers with 619 area codes will change to area code 760 in March 1997.

Anza-Borrego Desert State Park
Palm Canyon Drive Borrego Springs, CA 92004
619-767-4205
For a spring wildflower update, send a stamped post card, addressed to yourself, in an envelope. Mail it to: Wildflowers, Anza-Borrego Desert State Park, P.O. Box 299, Borrego Springs, CA 92004-0299. Or call 619-767-4684.

Automobile Club of Southern California
Travel Publications Dept.
2601 S. Figueroa St., H075
Los Angeles, CA 90007
213-741-4183

BLM Barstow Resource Area
150 Coolwater Lane
Barstow, CA 92311-3221
619-255-8700

BLM Bishop Resource Area
785 N. Main Street, Suite E
Bishop, CA 93514
619-872-4881

BLM California Desert District
6221 Box Springs Blvd.
Riverside, CA 92507
909-697-5200

BLM El Centro Resource Area
1661 S. 4th Street
El Centro, CA 92243
619-337-4400

BLM Needles Resource Area
101 West Spikes Rd.
P.O. Box 888
Needles, CA 92363
619-326-7000

BLM Palm Springs/South Coast Resource Area
690 W. Garnet Ave.
P.O. Box 2000
North Palm Springs, CA 92258
619-251-4800

BLM Ridgecrest Resource Area
300 S. Richmond Rd.
Ridgecrest, CA 93555
619-384-5400

California Association of Four-Wheel Drive Clubs
3104 O Street #313
Sacramento, CA 95816
916-332-8890

California Desert Information Center
831 Barstow Road
Barstow, CA 92311
619-255-8760

Death Valley National Park
Death Valley, CA 92328
619-786-2331

Eastern California Museum
155 Grant Street
Box 206
Independence, CA 93526
619-878-0258

Eastern Sierra InterAgency Visitor Center
Junction of U.S. 395 and state Hwy. 136
P.O. Drawer R
Lone Pine, CA 93545
619-876-6222

Friends of the Mojave Road
Goffs Schoolhouse
P.O. Box 7
Essex, CA
92332-0007
619-733-4482

Inyo National Forest White Mountain Ranger Station
798 North Main Street
Bishop, CA 93514
619-873-2500

Inyo National Forest Mt. Whitney Ranger Station
P.O. Box 8
Lone Pine, CA 93545
619-876-6200

Jawbone OHV Visitor Center
P.O. Box D28111
Jawbone Canyon Road
Cantil, CA 93519
619-373-1146

Joshua Tree National Park
74485 National Monument Drive
Twentynine Palms, CA 92277
619-367-7511

DESTINET camp reservations
1-800-365-2267

Mojave Desert Information Ctr.
(Mojave National Preserve)
72157 Baker Blvd.

P.O. Box 241
Baker, CA 92309
619-733-4040
Hole-In-The-Wall Visitor Center
619-928-2572

Picacho State Recreation Area
P.O. Box 848
Winterhaven, CA 92283
619-393-3052

Providence Mountains State Recreation Area
Essex, CA 92332
805-942-0662

Red Rock Canyon State Park
RRC Box 26
Cantil, CA 93519
(No telephone)
Contact: Calif. Dept. of Parks and Recreation
High Desert District
1051 West Avenue M, Suite 201
Lancaster, CA 93534
805-942-0662

San Bernardino National Forest Big Bear Ranger Station
P.O. Box 290
Fawnskin, CA 92333
909-866-3437

Santa Rosa Mountains National Scenic Area Visitor Ctr.
51-500 Highway 74
Palm Desert, CA 92260
619-862-9984

Tread Lightly!
298 24th Street
Suite 325-C
Ogden, UT 84401
1-800-966-9900

Glossary

Here are explanations of some terms and abbreviations that I use to describe what you'll see along the drives in this book.

Alluvial fan — A broad, fan-shaped slope of rock, gravel, sand, silt and soil deposited where a stream exits onto a plain from a canyon or gorge.

Anticline — A convex, or arched, fold in layered rock.

BLM — Bureau of Land Management, an agency of the U.S. Department of Interior. It manages millions of acres of federal public land.

Cairn — Rocks deliberately piled up to serve as a trail marker.

C.G. — Campground.

Desert pavement — Flat ground consisting of a layer of closely packed stones.

Desert varnish — A dark coating of iron and manganese that commonly covers desert rocks.

Fault — A fracture in the Earth's crust accompanied by a displacement of one side of the fracture with respect to the other and in a direction parallel to the fracture.

Geoglyph — A large, ancient ground design made by native people. There are two basic types, intaglios and rock alignments. Intaglios were made by moving surface rocks to reveal the lighter ground underneath. Rock alignments involved placing rocks into particular designs.

Graben — A depressed segment of the Earth's crust produced by subsidence between at least two faults.

N.P. — National park.

Petroglyph — A design deliberately etched into the thin, dark varnish that commonly covers desert rock.

Playa — A usually dry lake bed.

Sedimentary rock — Rock formed by accumulated sediments.

SRA — State recreation area.

Stratified — Layered, or sheetlike, rock or earth of one kind lying between beds of other kinds.

Tank — A natural rock basin where water collects.

Tufa — Porous deposits of calcium carbonate usually formed around hot springs, and around springs and lakes with high mineral content.

Wash — A dry streambed.

Wilderness — Once just a sparsely or unpopulated place dominated by nature, the 1964 Wilderness Act made it a legal designation as well. It is now defined, in part, as land that appears to be in a natural state, where the impact of humans is essentially unnoticeable. They are protected from consumptive uses, such as mining and logging, by humans. No forms of mechanized travel are allowed.

References
&
suggested reading

Adventuring in the California Desert, by Lynne Foster; San Francisco, CA: Sierra Club Books, 1987. An outstanding multi-activity guide to understanding and experiencing the desert. Includes some four-wheel-drive routes.

Bureau of Land Management Back Country Byways, by Stewart M. Green; Helena and Billings, MT: Falcon Press Publishing Co., 1991. Describes 38 drives in the West that the BLM has identified as having particular scenic, historic and cultural value.

Bureau of Land Management Desert Access Guides. There are 22 of them covering the BLM's California Desert District. They will need to be updated in the wake of the 1994 California Desert Protection Act.

Cadillac Desert; The American West and its Disappearing Water, by Marc Reisner; New York, N.Y.: Penguin Books, 1987. A highly readable, well-documented book about the extraordinary effort and expense required for large populations to exist in the arid West.

California Deserts, by Jerry Schad; Helena and Billings, MT: Falcon Press Publishing Co., 1988. Photographs with text describing the region.

California's Eastern Sierra; A Visitor's Guide, by Sue Irwin; Los Olivos, CA: Cachuma Press, 1991. A beautifully illustrated, well–written and informative full-color book that is an essential companion.

Congressional Quarterly, October 8, 1994, "Despite Senate Delays, Passage of Desert Bill Appears Likely;" and October 15, 1994, "Desert Bill Became a Trial In Crucial Final Hours." Both by Catalina Camia.

East of the High Sierra; The Ancient Bristlecone Pine Forest, by Russ and Anne Johnson; Bishop, CA: Sierra Media, Inc., 1970. Describes the White Mountains and trees that are among the oldest living things on Earth.

Exploring Death Valley, by Ruth Kirk; Stanford, CA: Stanford University Press, 1981. What to do, where to go, what to see.

Geology of the Sierra Nevada, by Mary Hill; Berkeley & Los Angeles; University of California Press, 1995.

Ghost Towns & Mining Camps of California; A History & Guide, by Remi Nadeau; Santa Barbara, CA: Crest Publishers, 1992. A good reference to help you appreciate early California history.

Titus Canyon Road Guide; A Tour Through Time, by Roger G. Brandt; Death Valley, CA: Death Valley Natural History Association, 1992. A detailed guide that will help you understand the history and geology along a spectacular drive in Death Valley National Park.

Mojave Road Guide, by Dennis G. Casebier and the Friends of the Mojave Road; Essex, CA: Tales of the Mojave Road Publishing Co., 1986. This is the definitive guide to the historic route. It is essential to fully and more safely experiencing the 138–mile road.

The Anza-Borrego Desert Region, by Lowell and Diana Lindsay. Berkeley: Wilderness Press, 1991. This is a detailed guide to a unique state park and adjacent areas. Includes a map.

Index

Photo index

Common desert plants

Ocotillo

Creosote bush

Yucca

Cholla cactus